HISPANIC AMERICAN PROFILES

Formerly entitled *The Illustrated Hispanic American Profiles*

GENE MACHAMER

Illustrations by Gene Machamer

ONE WORLD

BALLANTINE BOOKS | NEW YORK

A One World Book
Published by Ballantine Books

http://www.randomhouse.com

Library of Congress Catalog Card Number: 96-96535

ISBN 0-345-40423-8

Text design by Ann Gold

Manufactured in the United States of America
First Ballantine Books Edition: September 1996
10 9 8 7 6 5 4 3 2 1

DEDICATED TO ALL WHO TRY!
Also a special thanks to the librarians of
the Mechanicsburg, West Shore, and the
Pennsylvania State libraries . . .
I couldn't have made it without them!

CONTENTS

Those who cannot remember the past are
condemned to repeat it.

—*George Santayana*

What a great language I have, it's a fine language
we inherited from the fierce Conquistàdors. . . .
They carried everything off and left us everything. . . .
They left us the words.

—*Pablo Neruda*

INTRODUCTION

Mexican American. Cuban American. Puertoriqueño and Puertoriqueña. Latino and Latina. Chicano and Chicana. Hispano-Iberian American. In *Hispanic American Profiles*, the life stories of over 150 role models who have made enduring contributions which influenced every aspect of American life are featured. Regardless of whether they are well-known or lesser-known, these influential individuals have enriched the quality and diversity of our culture.

In a culture as ethnically diverse as ours, is it possible, or even desirable, to have an umbrella term under which all these groups can fit? We can't provide a simple answer to this complex question. What we can tell you is why we chose to use "Hispanic American" to describe the subjects of these mini-biographies.

So, what does "Hispanic" mean? Grace Flores-Hughes (whose profile appears on page 95), the Chairman of the Executive Board of the *Harvard Journal on Hispanic Policy*, asked the same question we did. In her article "Why the Term Hispanic?" Ms. Flores-Hughes says that she believes "Hispanic" is the best identification because, "it denotes only those peoples *whose origins are of Spanish lineage*." While other terms like "Spanish speaking" and "Spanish surname" have also been proposed for use by various government agencies, those choices have been discounted because language and surnames are not guarantees that a person is of Spanish origin.

"Hispanic" may be the most inclusive term, but in *Hispanic American Profiles* we are not attempting to paint everyone of Spanish lineage with broad strokes. We don't want to apply a single coat that masks the very real, and very important linguistic, cultural, religious, and geographic differences among the individuals profiled in this book.

The entries in this book are divided geographically to highlight the diverse origins of our accomplished subjects. Within each geographical category, we also present the broad range of contributions Hispanic Americans have made by occupation—including the arts and sciences, business and politics, sports and the military. We also hope that this arrangement will encourage readers to learn more about each of the countries, territories, and regions from which these extraordinary individuals came.

So much has been said and written about diversity and multi-culturalism in the last twenty years, that sometimes our words build walls instead of bridges. It is our hope that *Hispanic American Profiles* will be one of many bridges that remind us that although our differences and similarities are important, what matters most is what our unique gifts allow us to contribute to our collective cultural heritage.

THE OLD WORLD

SPAIN AND PORTUGAL

ELENA CASTEDO
Writer
(1937–   )

Elena Castedo was born in Barcelona, Spain. Her family fled the country while Castedo was still just a child, and settled in Chile, where she grew up.

Upon moving north to the United States, Castedo entered the University of California at Los Angeles and earned her master of arts degree. Later, she received a Ph.D. from Howard University.

Castedo has edited the *Inter-America Review of Bibliography* and has written a book on Chilean theater, but she is probably best known for her first novel, *Paradise*. The main characters in the book are the mother and her nine-year-old daughter, Solita. Ms. Castedo makes Solita the narrator of the story, a tale of escaping the 1930s world of Franco's Spain. Literary critics praise the book, saying *Paradise* is not just another American novel with identifiably American symbols, themes, and characters. It is a unique hybrid of the best of America and Latin America combined.

Castedo's first novel, which was a National Book Award nominee, should be read as a sensitive, almost lyrical incursion into human motivation as perceived by a child.

Elena Castedo now lives in Virginia and continues to write novels.

JOSÉ DE RIVERA
Sculptor
(1904–1985)

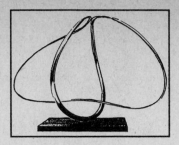

Born in West Baton Rouge, Louisiana, the son of a sugar mill engineer, Rivera learned the skills of a sculptor at an early age when he used the tools on his father's farm.

Though he had no formal art training, Rivera worked for eight years in factories and in foundries with tools and dies. He became an adept blacksmith and master machinist.

Between 1928 and 1931 Rivera studied drawing under the painter John Norton at the studio school in Chicago. Soon after, he decided to become a professional artist and traveled throughout Europe and Egypt, studying and drawing. He was influenced by Belgian artist and theorist Georges Vantongerloo.

Finally, after a year of traveling through Europe visiting galleries and museums in 1932, Rivera reaffirmed his decision to be a sculptor. His first exhibited sculptures in the 1930s were machine-age stylizations made from sheets of steel. By the mid-1940s he had switched to the linear, arabesque forms for which he is best known.

In the 1950s, his style centered on working with steel rods that he forged and hammered into gleaming, polished curves that described space and simplicity.

Rivera has won many awards. His work is in many major American museums, as well as the Tate Gallery in London. In 1938 he constructed the aluminum *Flight* for Newark Airport.

GEORGE MENDOZA
Author
(1934–   )

A native New Yorker born to an Irish mother and Spanish father in 1934, George Mendoza moved to Long Island with his family at an early age. He received a prep school education and learned how to sail. He survived a boating incident on Long Island Sound that could have been fatal when both his rudder and the centerboard broke on his sloop, and he lost the jib. He was drifting out to sea when a yacht saw his distress signal and rescued him.

Mendoza attended Columbia University, where he honed his writing skills as an English and creative writing major. He also perfected his sailing skills at the State Maritime College at Fort Schuyler and blended his two loves with a couple of solo transatlantic voyages during each of which he completed a novel. The ocean, he says, stirs his imagination and allows him to work without interruption. Mendoza also is an award-winning poet and author of children's books. His work reflects a commitment to issues such as injustice and the plight of the underprivileged. Other themes found in his books are loneliness, the power of man's imagination, and the mystique of the ocean.

Mendoza is married and has a daughter. His books include *And Amedeo Asked, How Does One Become a Man?*; *The Puma and the Pearl*; *The Hunter I Might Have Been*; *The Crack in the Wall and Other Terribly Weird Tales*; and *The Inspector*.

GEORGE SANTAYANA
Philosopher, Poet
(1863–1952)

George Santayana was born in Madrid, Spain, on December 16, 1863. At the age of nine, he moved with his mother to Boston, where he enrolled in the Boston Latin School. Santayana received his B.A. and Ph.D. from Harvard University, then went to teach philosophy there from 1889 until 1912. Santayana published his first books of poetry and philosophical essays while at Harvard. In 1905–06, he wrote perhaps his greatest work, the five-volume *Life of Reason*, which brought him international fame and on which generations of American naturalist philosophers were raised.

In 1912, Santayana inherited a small sum of money that enabled him to leave teaching and move to Europe, where he remained until his death. He devoted his life to philosophical reflection and literary work. Though Spanish was his native tongue, all of his literary works were written in English.

Santayana's famous quote—"Those who cannot remember the past are condemned to repeat it"—illustrates his thoughts on the meaning of life's experiences. He looked to the past to help him understand the present and future.

Santayana's published work included books of poetry, philosophical and autobiographical works, novels, and books of short stories.

Santayana died in Rome in 1952 at the age of eighty-nine.

AL (FONSO RAMON) LOPEZ

Baseball Player, Manager
(1908–1992)

Al Lopez was born in Ybor City, the Spanish-speaking section of Tampa, Florida, on August 20, 1908. His parents had moved there from Madrid, Spain, to find work in the cigar trade. Because of peer pressure, young Lopez learned to speak Spanish before English. He also learned to hate the odor of the cigar factories and vowed he would work elsewhere. At sixteen, he left school to play with the Tampa Smokers. During an exhibition game his first year, he caught the legendary pitcher Walter Johnson, who complimented him on his skills.

He rose through the minors and was called up by the Brooklyn Dodgers in 1930, playing well enough to make the 1934 All-Star team. Other National League teams for whom he played were the Boston Bees and the Pittsburgh Pirates. In 1947, he was traded to the American League Cleveland Indians. As a player through eighteen seasons, he caught 1,918 games, which set a major-league record.

In 1938, he began his second baseball career as a manager with Indianapolis for three years, leading that American Association team to a first-place and two second-place finishes. For six seasons after that, he managed the Cleveland Indians, then later managed the Chicago White Sox, leading them to the pennant in 1959, their first in forty years, and earning himself Manager of the Year honors in the American League.

Lopez was married and had a son. His favorite recreational sports were hunting, fishing, and golf. He passed away in 1992.

Paul H. Alvarez

Business Executive

(1942–   )

Paul H. Alvarez is chairman, president, and chief executive officer of Ketchum Communications, parent company of several advertising and sales promotion companies. He is a member of the board of directors and the executive committee of Ketchum Communications.

He assumed the title of president and chief executive officer in 1992, and was elected chairman of the board in 1993. Mr. Alvarez joined Ketchum in 1971 as an account supervisor of Ketchum Public Relations following positions at Rockwell International, PPG Industries, and Burston-Marsteller. He subsequently held positions as director of Ketchum Public Relations' Los Angeles office, director of consumer public relations, executive vice president in charge of new business, and chairman/chief executive officer of the company.

In 1990, he was named vice chairman of Ketchum Communications and also held the title of president of Ketchum Specialized Services, which included oversight for all Ketchum holding companies except Advertising and International.

Mr. Alvarez is treasurer of the Pittsburgh council board of governors of the American Association of Advertising Agencies and a member of its national board, and an accredited member and fellow of the Public Relations Society of America, for which he has served as chairman of public relations. He also serves as a member of the board of various civic organizations, and co-chaired a committee that developed a model curriculum for graduate school education in public relations.

ALEX ARMENDARIS
Business Advocate
(1930–1992)

Born and raised in Chicago, Alex Armendaris joined the U.S. Navy in 1950 and served four years, including a combat tour in the Korean War.

He became involved in politics during the 1964 presidential campaign of Arizona Senator Barry Goldwater, later becoming chairman of the Indiana Young Republicans. Six year later, he headed the victorious congressional campaign for New York's Republican Jack Kemp. In the same year, his newly formed management firm signed on to work for President Nixon.

In 1977, he left government politics and entered the field of marketing. His company, Market Growth, was one of the first of its kind to target Hispanic business ventures. He ran two marketing firms until 1989. He took leave from his companies in 1980 and 1981 to assist the Republican presidential campaign, where he served as the political director for Hispanic outreach. Armendaris later served as associate director of White House personnel under President Reagan.

Taking on another assignment, he became special assistant for public affairs to Mr. Horace Deets, the executive director of the American Association of Retired Persons. He held that position until he died, December 3, 1992.

Alex Armendaris will always be known for his compassion and understanding in helping Hispanic business communities develop nationwide.

JOSEPH A. UNANUE

President of
Goya Foods, Inc.
(1925–   )

President Joseph Unanue worked for Goya Foods, the nation's largest Hispanic food company, for twenty-five years before being named head of the Secaucus, New Jersey, company founded by his parents, Don Prudencio Unanue and Dona Carolina Casal Unanue, in 1936.

Following service in the U.S. Army during World War II, the Brooklyn-born Mr. Unanue received a degree in mechanical engineering from the Catholic University of America in Washington, D.C. He then joined his father at Goya Foods.

Working with his brother Frank, president of Goya de Puerto Rico, Mr. Unanue has fostered a new era in which Goya's reputation for high quality has grown beyond the loyal audience of Hispanic and Caribbean consumers. Over 800 Goya products attract new devotees each day, supplied by an extensive international operation with packing plants in Puerto Rico, the Dominican Republic, Spain, and New Jersey. Goya also maintains distribution centers in several U.S. cities.

While Goya Foods supports hundreds of civic, cultural, athletic, and religious organizations, Mr. Unanue himself has been honored repeatedly for his community-minded service. He has been named Man of the Year twice by the National Conference of Christians and Jews and, in 1991, received the National Hispanic Achievement Award, which was presented by *Hispanic Magazine*.

Goya Foods sales reach an excess of $400 million per year, with a staff of more than 800 workers.

VICENTE MARTINEZ YBOR

Cigar Manufacturer
(1818–1896)

Born in Spain in 1818, Vicente Martinez Ybor immigrated first to Cuba and then to Key West, Florida, where he established himself as a manufacturer of cigars. When two Spanish friends came to Florida to search in vain for wild mango and guava groves to use for producing Spanish delicacies, they did spot an excellent site near Tampa for a cigar factory and told Ybor about it.

Ybor, dissatisfied with his Key West location, came to take a look and agreed that this would be his ideal site—one with an excellent climate, lots of fresh water, and easily accessible by both land and sea. So he acquired forty acres and began to construct not only his factory buildings but an entire town. Tampa officials welcomed help in the rebuilding of the area after the ravages of the Civil War and granted him complete planning control of what was to be called Ybor City.

Ybor offered Hispanic and other workers inexpensive housing with their jobs, and he lured investors and manufacturers with free land and quality buildings. Hispanics were later joined by Italian immigrants. The city prospered, but the Cuban revolution in the 1890s split the Spanish and Cuban workers into hostile factions. Strikes and demonstrations became the order of the day. Even Ybor's funeral could not unite the workers, who mourned as separate ethnic and political groups.

This division persisted for generations and hindered the realization of its founder's dream for a real community in Ybor City, which eventually became part of Tampa.

DENNIS CHAVEZ
Political Leader
(1888–1962)

Dennis Chavez was born in Los Chavez, New Mexico, a town named for his ancestors. The family ranch originated with a 1769 grant from Spain's king, and a Chavez relative had become the first governor of New Mexico after Spain had ceded the territory to Mexico in 1821.

One of eight kids in a poor family, Dennis had to drop out of school after eighth grade to earn money driving a grocery wagon. A voracious reader, he enjoyed the works of Thomas Jefferson, and by seventeen, was set on a government career. He knew he needed more education, so when he became Spanish interpreter for A. A. Jones, New Mexico's U.S. senator, he enrolled at Georgetown University. He had to pass a special test as a non–high school graduate. Armed with a law degree and years of experience as a legislative aide, he returned to Albuquerque and set up a law practice. Then he won a seat in the legislature and, in 1930, a seat in Congress. He lost a close race in 1934 for U.S. Senate, but a year later was appointed to fill that seat when the winner died in a plane crash. That made Chavez the Senate's first Hispanic member. He won a special election in 1936 and held that Senate seat until his death in 1962.

He championed Hispanic and Indian causes, fought ethnic and racial discrimination, and probed poverty in Puerto Rico. With his trademark cigar, Senator Chavez was a popular and easygoing man but a tough fighter for his favorite causes in the Senate and in the Democratic National Committee platform deliberations.

LINDA CHAVEZ
Political Leader
(1947–   )

Linda Chavez was born in Albuquerque, New Mexico, on June 17, 1947. She has devoted her life to public service, concentrating on the areas of civil and human rights. *The New York Times* has said that Linda is "an influential voice on civil rights policy."

Chavez is currently head of the Center for the New American Community, which seeks to foster a renewed commitment to a common American civic culture and a shared identity among the diverse people who make up this nation. She has held numerous political positions, including White House director of public liaison (1985). In this capacity, she was the highest-ranking woman on the White House staff. As staff director of the U.S. Commission on Civil Rights (1983–1985), Chavez directed studies on discrimination based on race, sex, national origin, religion, age, and handicap.

Chavez is the author of *Out of the Barrio: Toward a New Politics of Hispanic Assimilation*, which chronicles Hispanic progress and achievement, and addresses the implications of bilingual education, voting rights, immigration policy, and affirmative action.

Chavez is known to many from her regular appearances on PBS's *To the Contrary*, CNN's *Crier & Co.*, and as a 1992 election commentator for *The MacNeil-Lehrer Newshour*. She has also appeared on numerous network shows, including *Good Morning America*, the *Today* show, *Phil Donahue*, and *Geraldo*.

HENRY G. CISNEROS
Leader
(1947–)

A descendant on his father's side of early Spanish settlers in the Southwest, Henry Gabriel Cisneros was born in San Antonio, Texas, in 1947. In college, Henry became interested in urban planning, earned a bachelor's and a master's degree from Texas A&M University, a Ph.D. from George Washington University, and a second master's degree from Harvard University, this one in public administration, and was a White House Fellow, among other early achievements.

In 1974, Cisneros returned to San Antonio with his wife and child. A year later, he won an uphill race to become the youngest person ever to serve on city council there. Six years later, he ran for mayor and won. He set out to encourage tourism, conventions, and high tech industries to come to San Antonio.

Although some Hispanic critics did not think him activist enough, Cisneros's moderate policies helped ease ethnic tensions and attracted new jobs to the area. The first time he was re-elected, he garnered more than 90 percent of the vote. He also faced some setbacks, like voter rejection of a bond issue he had deemed important.

But he drew national attention. He was president of the National League of Cities and was considered a possible Democratic vice presidential candidate in 1984.

On December 17, 1992, President Clinton appointed Cisneros as secretary of the Department of Housing and Urban Development.

BERNARDO DE GÁLVEZ
Leader
(1746–1786)

Born in Macharaviaya, Spain, in 1746, Bernardo de Gálvez served with the Spanish army in its war with Portugal and in New Spain battling the Apaches. He was appointed governor of the province of Louisiana in 1776.

He liked the British as little as the breakaway colonists did, recognizing that their bases near Louisiana threatened Spanish interests. When the Revolutionary War broke out, he wanted Spain also to declare war on the British so they would be forced to return western Florida and the eastern side of the Mississippi, territory Gálvez believed rightfully should belong to Spain.

He provided cover for Americans moving gunpowder from New Orleans to Fort Pitt and protected ships carrying colonists' trade goods to Europe from British attacks. In 1779, Gálvez received battle orders from Madrid. He led successful raids against the British in Florida, Baton Rouge, and Mobile, the latter battle fought with the assistance of marines from Cuba.

Soon, the only British base left on the Gulf of Mexico was at Pensacola, a well-manned outpost. It took Gálvez a year to muster a 7,000-man force and plan his strategy. In 1781, after several days of severe fighting, the British surrendered. This victory represented the peak of Spanish power here, with Spanish territory stretching from Florida to San Francisco.

The Bay of Galveston is named for this soldier-politician, who in his final years became viceroy of Mexico and helped to shape Spanish policy in this part of the world.

MANUEL LISA

Pioneer Explorer, Trader
(1772–1820)

Born in New Orleans in 1772, Manuel Lisa arrived in St. Louis when he was eighteen armed with an overweening ambition to develop a trading empire out in the unexplored frontier and a willingness to work hard to achieve that goal. He also had a knack for alienating people, making lots of enemies in his short but fruitful life.

He had gotten a Spanish patent on monopoly trade with the Osage Indians, but Governor James Wilkinson wouldn't let him use St. Louis as a home base for trade with the Spanish in Santa Fe. So when Lewis and Clark explored the upper Missouri River in their 1803 expedition, Lisa moved in that direction. He launched a 42-man expedition of his own up the Missouri into central Montana, set up a makeshift Manuel's Fort, and used that as a base for further explorations. He was looking for a back way to get to Santa Fe and engage in then-illegal trade with the Spanish, but that was not to be. Instead, Lisa began trading with the Indian tribes in the region. In 1809, with other traders, he created the Missouri Fur Company, which did well at first, then ran into trouble because of the hostility of some Indians, accidental fires, and interference by a suspicious government.

Lisa, however, was an important source of intelligence about the frontier, and eventually became an Indian agent for the United States, successfully converting the Sioux to allies. He put up Fort Lisa, near Omaha, as the base of his company and became known as a founder of Old Nebraska. He led thirteen trips into unexplored territory and died at age forty-eight.

JOSEPH MONTOYA

Former U.S. Senator
(1915–   )

Joseph Montoya, a former U.S. senator from New Mexico, has worked in government for over forty years. Joseph was born in Pena Blanca, New Mexico, in 1915. His ancestors were among the early Spanish settlers of that area. In 1931 he entered Regis College. After three years he transferred to Georgetown University Law School in Washington, D.C.

While in law school, Joseph supported himself by working for the Interior Department and was also elected to the New Mexico house of representatives. In 1938 Mr. Montoya received his law degree and was reelected to the state house of representatives. He was elected to the state senate in 1940 and the U.S. House of Representatives in 1957.

Joseph Montoya became a U.S. senator in 1964. He has always worked hard for education, housing, and the protection of our environment. He became nationally known as a member of the Senate Committee that investigated Watergate. The committee hearings were shown on network television during the summer of 1973.

SEVERO OCHOA

Biochemist, Physician,
Professor
(1905–1993)

Born in Luarca, Spain, on September 24, 1905, Severo Ochoa earned an A.B. degree in Málaga and his M.D. degree, with honors, at the University of Madrid. He chose not to practice medicine but to pursue work in the life sciences.

His career was capped as co-winner (with Arthur Kornberg) of the Nobel Prize for Medicine in 1959 for the research he directed as chairman of the Biochemistry Department at New York University College of Medicine into RNA (ribonucleic acid), which has helped to break the genetic code of life.

After college, he worked in Glasgow and at several institutes in Germany before returning to the University of Madrid as a lecturer and later head of the physiology division of its Institute for Medical Research. But research opportunities there were too narrow and he went to work in England and Germany. He accepted an offer in St. Louis in 1941 and joined the NYU staff a year later.

His earlier work included research on vitamin B^1 and numerous studies into enzymes, as a result of which he was credited with a number of important breakthroughs. Worldwide honors he received included honorary degrees and professorships, prestigious invitations to lecture, and such awards as the Newberg Medal in Biochemistry, the award of the Societé de Chimie Biologique, and the Borden Award in the Medical Sciences of the Association of American Colleges.

Dr. Ochoa became an American citizen in 1956 but returned to Spain in 1986 to finish out the rest of his life.

ELWOOD RICHARD QUESADA
Federal Aviation Pioneer
(1904–1993)

Quesada was born on April 13, 1904, in Washington, D.C. He attended Washington public grade and high schools. He later studied at Wyoming Seminary in Kingston, Pennsylvania, the University of Maryland, and Georgetown University. In 1924 he joined the army as a private, became a flying cadet, and later was commissioned as a regular army officer in the Air Corps.

In 1929, he was relief pilot on the monoplane *Question Mark*, which remained aloft over San Diego for over six days, an endurance record proving the efficacy of air refueling. For this feat, the crew were awarded the Distinguished Flying Cross. When the army flew the air mail (1933–34), he was chief pilot of the New York–Cleveland route.

In 1943, he was named commanding general of the 12th Fighter Command. Popular with his men, he was referred to as the the "pilots' general." Quesada flew more than ninety combat missions, many of them in the North African and Italian campaigns. Transferred to England as commander of the 9th Fighter Group, he directed the U.S. air effort before and during the invasion of Normandy.

Quesada returned to Washington after the war in Europe and was assigned as assistant chief of air staff for intelligence. In 1946 he took over the Tactical Air Command, and in October 1947 was promoted to lieutenant general.

Quesada retired from the military in 1951. From 1953 to 1955 he was vice president of Lockheed Aircraft. On June 14, 1957, President Eisenhower appointed him special assistant for aviation facilities planning, and in 1958 nominated him to be head of the Federal Aviation Agency.

PABLO CASALS

Violoncellist, Conductor, Composer
(1876–1973)

For over seventy years, Pablo Casals thrilled music lovers with his brilliant playing of the cello, his music composition, and his conducting.

Casals was born in Vendrell, a village about forty miles from Barcelona, Spain, on December 29, 1876. He began studying the cello in Barcelona at the early age of eleven, having already mastered the piano, violin, and organ. Later, in Madrid, he studied music with the help of a scholarship from Spain's Queen Christina. Casals and his mother moved to Belgium and then Paris to continue his studies. In 1899, at the age of twenty-three, Casals made his debut in Paris. He went on to become famous throughout the world.

Fiercely opposed to General Francisco Franco's Fascist rule in Spain, Casals vowed never to return to his native land while Franco remained in power. During his exile he lived first in France, then in Puerto Rico, his mother's birthplace, where he remained until his death.

Casals traveled often to the United States to give recitals. After performing at the White House for President Kennedy, he and Kennedy became close friends.

In 1954, the German writer Thomas Mann, himself one of the greatest artists of the twentieth century, said, "For me as for thousands of others, his very existence is a source of joy."

Casals died at the age of ninety-six, never having returned to his beloved Spain.

THE NEW WORLD

CENTRAL AND SOUTH AMERICA

ISABEL ALLENDE
Author
(1942–   )

Born in 1942 in Lima, Peru, where her father, a Chilean diplomat, was posted, Isabel Allende survived an array of problems to become a major Latin American novelist. Her parents divorced, a 1973 military coup violently ended the regime of her uncle, President Salvador Allende of Chile, and the ensuing repressions forced her family to escape to Venezuela.

Her first book, *The House of the Spirits*, was resisted by publishers in Latin America both because of its length and a traditional bias against women writers. It was originally published in Spain in the early 1980s and then was reprinted a few years later in the United States. Several other novels followed, tracing the lives and fortunes of a fictional Chilean family caught up in the fate of the nation itself, and capturing what one critic called "the tormented patriarchal world of traditional Hispanic society."

In her younger years, Allende had lived in various countries with her mother and diplomat stepfather. As an adult, she has worked for the UN Food and Agriculture Organization, conducted interviews on TV, and helped with movie newsreels; she also wrote articles for a feminist magazine, as well as plays and children's stories, and became a wife and mother. The political downfall and death of her uncle, the first man ever chosen to head a Marxist government through a free multiparty election, a coup in which the United States reportedly was involved, proved a turning point in her life.

Isabel Allende, who speaks English fluently, has lived and worked in America as well.

FERNANDO KRAHN
Author, Illustrator
(1935–   )

Born in Santiago, Chile, in 1935, Fernando Krahn was raised in a family who nurtured his creative abilities. He pored over his father's childhood books, which had been preserved by his German grandmother. His mother was a soprano who enjoyed singing opera, and his father, an attorney by profession, wrote operettas, arranged touring summer circuses that involved the family, and was a fine amateur cartoonist.

Though he studied law for several years, Fernando's major interests took him in a different direction. He left the university to become a stage designer and won second place in a Paris competition. But he had a portfolio of cartoons that he was anxious to test in the New York marketplace, so he headed there. He made sales to such prestigious magazines as *Esquire*, *The Atlantic Monthly*, *The New Yorker*, *Horizon*, and the *Reporter*. He became the *Reporter*'s exclusive cartoonist until the magazine's demise.

He married the Chilean author, playwright, and educator Maria de la Luz Uribe and they have three children. At the peak of his career, he took his family to live in Spain and began concentrating on illustrated children's books along with his adult cartoons. He even has experimented with film animation techniques. His books include *Journeys of Sebastian*, *Hildegarde and Maximilian*, and *A Funny Friend from Heaven*. He has also illustrated books by his wife and other authors.

MARISOL
Sculptor
(1930–   )

Marisol Escobar, born in Paris, France, to wealthy Venezuelan parents, moved to New York City in 1950 to study at the Art Students League. Her early works depict her interest in pre-Columbian art. Later, her sculptures and figurines began to reflect her eccentric personality.

Marisol has created many large pieces, probably the most famous being *The Party* (1965–66), which consists of life-sized figures. Marisol created the bodies from solid blocks of wood, then decorated them with bits and pieces of her own clothing. Another famous sculpture, *Mi Mama y Yo*, has been exhibited around the world, but is kept in Marisol's personal possession.

Marisol's works were displayed largely in group shows until 1958, when she had her first one-woman show at a New York gallery. Many of her sculptures were exhibited at the National Portrait Gallery in Washington, D.C., in 1991. In addition, her American Merchant Mariners Monument stands tribute to sailors everywhere on a breakwater off Manhattan.

Her art is now housed in the world's greatest museums, including the Metropolitan Museum of Art and the Museum of Modern Art in New York City.

Marisol still resides in New York.

FELIPE ALOU

Major League Baseball
Player, Manager
(1935–   )

Born in Haina, Dominican Republic, on May 12, 1935, Alou had a brilliant seventeen-year career in the majors, starting with San Francisco in 1958 and ending in 1974 at Milwaukee. History was made in September 1963, when he appeared in the same Giants outfield with younger brothers Jesus and Matty.

In 1964, Alou was traded to the Braves and led the National League in hits (218), runs (122), and total bases (355) and was named to the post-season All-Star team. Retiring with a career average of .286, he became the 31st player in history with at least 2,000 hits and 200 homers.

Alou has been a member of the Montreal Expos' organization for twenty years. He made his debut with the Expos as an invited instructor at spring training '76 in Daytona Beach. He managed A-West Palm Beach in 1977 and again for six seasons, 1986–91. Also, he managed in the Winter Leagues for twelve seasons, winning the Caribbean World Series in 1990 at Escogido of the Dominican League.

Alou compiled an impressive twelve-year minor-league managerial mark of 844–751 (.541). His teams finished first three times and won two championships. In 1990, he was named Manager of the Year in the Florida State League, with a 92–40 record, an all-time franchise high for wins.

The Montreal Expos named Alou as manager on May 22, 1992. He became the first Dominican-born manager in major-league history, and is the fourth Latin American manager born in the islands. Tony Perez (Camaguey, Cuba) became the fifth when he was named to manage the Reds. Others are: Preston Gomez (Cuba), San Diego, Houston, and the Cubs; Mike Gonzalez (Cuba), Cardinals; and Cookie Rojas (Cuba), Angels.

ROBERTO GUERRERO
Indy Race Car Driver
(1958–   )

Born in Medillín, Colombia, November 16, 1958, young Roberto Guerrero began racing Go-Karts when he was twelve years old. Within two years, he was preparing his own engines and chassis and was claiming the first of two Colombian national karting championships.

One of Guerrero's most admirable traits on and off the track, determination, has been a telling factor in many aspects of his life. Earning valuable funds while attending college, he was able to attend the Jim Russell School of Motor Racing.

In the late seventies and early eighties, he worked his way up the racing ladder, including eight British Formula Ford victories. The '84 burst that Guerrero made onto the Indy Car scene was anything but modest. Driving for the Master Mechanic Tools team, he debuted with a twenty-sixth-place finish at Long Beach, and a second place to Rick Mears, earning a share of the Rookie of the Year honors.

The 1987 season was one of triumph and tragedy for Roberto and Katie Guerrero. After he won at Phoenix and Mid-Ohio, a second Indy 500 runner-up trophy made him a name to beat. Then a crash during a test session left Roberto in a coma and Katie standing vigil by his hospital bed for days.

Incredibly, Guerrero rebounded from his injuries to reclaim the cockpit of Vince Granatelli's racer in 1988. In 1992, he rejoined with Indy Car team owner and drag racer Kenny Bernstein. During a qualification lap at Indy, he set a lap record at 232.482 mph.

Guerrero states, "With my continued association with Kenny Bernstein and our new association with Budweiser, I have never found a better home as a driver."

JUAN MARICHAL
Baseball Pitcher
(1937–   )

Marichal was born October 20, 1937, in Laguna Verde, Dominican Republic. He was signed out of the Dominican Air Force at the age of nineteen. The high-kicking pitcher already had pinpoint control of his curve, slider, screwball, and blinding fastball, all thrown with a variety of motions.

He led the 1958 Midwest League and the 1959 Eastern League in wins and ERA. When he debuted with the Giants on July 19, 1960, he shut out the Phillies on one hit. Marichal teamed with Gaylord Perry to give the San Francisco Giants a fear-inspiring duo.

Marichal led the National League in wins, innings, shutouts, and complete games twice each and in ERA, strikeouts, and winning percentage once each. He won at least twenty-five games in a season three times. He never won a Cy Young Award, mainly because his best years coincided with the peak years of Sandy Koufax. His great career lasted fifteen years.

Tempers always flared between the Giants and the Dodgers, but on August 22, 1965, one of the most violent brawls in major-league history erupted. Marichal had flattened two Dodgers, and when he came to bat, the Dodgers' catcher, Johnny Roseboro, came close to Marichal's head with the return throw. An argument ensued and Marichal hit the catcher on the head with his bat. The rest is history.

When Marichal was not named to the Hall of Fame in his first two years of eligibility, Roseboro campaigned for his election and received a special thanks at Marichal's induction ceremony in 1983.

GABRIELA SABATINI
Tennis Star
(1970–   )

Born in Buenos Aires, Argentina, in 1970, Gabriela Sabatini began hitting a tennis ball against a wall when she was six years old. Her father, director of GM's Argentine operations, enrolled her in a tennis club a year later. Within three years, she was ranked first in Argentina's under-twelve girls division. After only one year of junior high, she was sent to Key Biscayne, Florida, to train with former Chilean Davis Cup player Patricio Apey.

In 1984, Sabatini became the youngest player ever to reach the final sixteen at the U.S. Open. Under professional management, she endorsed a line of fashion tennis wear and turned pro, quickly establishing herself as a threat by beating ranked players. She drove herself to improve her game through long practice sessions and a grueling schedule of tournaments. An early highlight of her career was her first-time upset of Steffi Graf to win the Virginia Slims of Florida title. Her father, who by now was her full-time manager, had switched coaches to Angel Gimenez, a former Spanish Davis Cup player, who honed her endurance and skills.

She won the silver medal at the 1988 Summer Olympics, then nailed down three major big-money championships. As her career took a roller-coaster course, she turned to still another trainer, former Brazilian player Carlos Kirmayr, who restructured her style of play. Two months later, she was an upset winner at the U.S. Open. A relentless competitor, she squared off against Mary Joe Fernandez in a 1993 match at the French Open that lasted three hours and thirty five minutes—the longest Women's Grand Slam match in history.

Sabatini is rated as one of the world's top women tennis players, and her on-court earnings are augmented by millions of dollars worth of endorsements.

ANDRES B. BANDE

Business Executive

(1944–   )

Mr. Bande was born July 10, 1944, in Santiago, Chile. He was president of Ameritech International, the global subsidiary of Ameritech developing and operating business opportunities worldwide in telecommunications-related areas.

Bande began his career as a lawyer in Chile, where he specialized in investment and insurance. From there, he joined a brokerage firm at Lloyds of London.

Appointed president in June 1990, Bande organized and launched Ameritech International and was responsible for managing the worldwide organization, based in Chicago. He brought to his post nearly a quarter of a century of experience in international telecommunications, having worked and traveled in more than a hundred countries.

Before joining Ameritech, Bande was executive vice president of U.S. West International, the regional Bell company headquartered in Denver. He reorganized the firm and was responsible for worldwide business activities and expanding U.S. West investments to six markets.

Extremely active in Hispanic and corporate organizations, Bande serves as a member of the board of directors of the Mexican American Legal Defense and Educational Fund. He also served as chairman of the President's Advisory Commission on Educational Excellence for Hispanic Americans.

Among his many achievements, Bande was listed among "The Corporate Elite" in 1993, a who's who of the top power players in the country according to *Hispanic Business Magazine*. He now works as a consultant.

OSCAR DE LA RENTA
Fashion Designer
(1932–   )

World-famous fashion designer Oscar de la Renta was born in Santo Domingo, Dominican Republic, on July 22, 1932. He began studying art in his homeland and completed his studies in Madrid, Spain, where he became interested in fashion design. It was in Madrid that Mrs. John Lodge, wife of the U.S. ambassador to Spain, saw de la Renta's sketches and commissioned him to design a gown for her daughter's debut. The daughter, wearing the gown, appeared on the cover of *Life* magazine.

De la Renta spent several years working for top fashion design houses, including Balenciaga, before moving to New York in 1963 to design for Elizabeth Arden. Early in 1965, he left Elizabeth Arden to buy into Jane Derby, which he eventually took over.

In 1967, de la Renta won the Coty Winnie, which is awarded to the designer chosen by a jury of fashion editors for having had the most significant influence on fashion for the past year. He received the Coty award again in 1968. Other fashion awards presented to de la Renta include the Neiman Marcus Award and Italy's Tiberio d'Oro. The Dominican Republic has awarded him the Order of Juan Pablo Duarte.

Known primarily for his aristocratic styling, de la Renta has also created fashions that are daring and provocative. His designs have been worn by the world's most famous women.

SHEILA GUARDERAS
Business Owner
(1961–)

The entrepreneurial spirit and business ingenuity of Sheila Guarderas has built Superior Services into a major competitor in today's service industry.

Born in Elmonte, California, and raised in Alaska, Ms. Guarderas aspired to follow in the footsteps of her self-made parents, Oscar and Irene, who built a thriving similar business in Alaska.

Capitalizing on the perseverance and spirit inherited from her parents, she proceeded to form her own business in 1986. Today her company is a multimillion-dollar operation, employing over 275 professionals throughout the western United States.

Ms. Guarderas currently serves as president-elect of the Central California Hispanic Chamber of Commerce, is a corporate adviser to the National Hispanic Student Network, and sits on the advisory committee for education on the U.S. Senate Task Force for Hispanic Affairs.

Exemplifying the spirit of the free enterprise system and outstanding leadership in the Hispanic community, she was presented the 1992 Women Entrepreneur of the Year Award from the U.S. Hispanic Chamber of Commerce. Successful business ventures have placed Superior Services among the top 500 Hispanic-owned businesses in the nation, according to *Hispanic Business Magazine*.

MARY RODAS
Business Consultant
(1975–)

Born on Christmas Day in 1975 to immigrant parents from El Salvador, Mary Rodas's rise to success has not been the typical one. At four years of age, while accompanying her father, Miguel, on his rounds as the assistant building superintendent, Rodas noticed that a man was improperly installing an apartment floor tile. From that moment on, she struck a lifelong bond with the inventor and founder of Catco, Inc., Donald Spector.

Serving as a consultant to numerous inventors, in 1989, Rodas became the vice president of marketing for Catco, a $70 million toy company. Quite an accomplishment for anyone at age thirteen.

Rodas introduced the Balzac Balloon Ball, creating an instant success in the toy industry and in the twenty-seven countries in which it is sold. Balzac stores will be opening all across the United States and in Europe in 1996. She will visit every store to be sure consumers know about and like her products.

In 1993, Rodas, with her vivid imagination and astute marketing eye, forayed into the music business and became vice president of A&R for Deco Disc Industries, a newly formed company. Her input includes the suggestion of die cuts and licensed characters to appeal to kids.

What's her future project? Rodas is lending her toy instincts to the candy industry to produce creative candy concoctions.

Mary Rodas understands the importance of family and education. She graduated from the Professional Children's School in 1994, and is currently attending New York University.

RUBÉN BLADES

Actor, Composer, Singer
(1948–)

In addition to being an international singer, composer, and actor, Rubén Blades has a master's degree in international law from Harvard University.

Blades taught himself to sing and play guitar by listening to the radio in his native Panama. While at the University of Panama, he played with an Afro-Cuban band. During the 1970s, he recorded and toured the United States with a salsa band. Blades's first solid hit came in 1984 with his recording of *Buscando America*, which was named one of *Time* magazine's ten best rock albums of the year.

Blades has appeared in several motion pictures, including *The Milagro Beanfield War*, has performed at Carnegie Hall, and won four Grammy Awards and numerous gold records.

In 1990, Blades and his band released *Rubén Blades y Son del Solar*. The *Daily News* of Los Angeles rated it suberb and stated that his style is just one example of Blades's forward-looking vision.

He ran unsuccessfully for president of Panama in 1994.

JERRY GARCIA
Composer, Guitarist
(1942–1995)

Born in San Francisco to a jazz musician father originally from Spain and a Swedish-Irish mother, Jerome John Garcia had a troubled childhood after his dad died. Though interested in art, literature, and music, Jerry grew rebellious, disliked school, palled around with a rowdy, hard-drinking crowd, and eventually enlisted in the army to escape.

Primarily self-taught, he became interested in the guitar and bluegrass banjo. He played with a group called Mother McCree's Uptown Jug Champions, which, after the Beatles' success, restructured itself as an electric blues group, The Warlocks, which was linked to the sixties' LSD drug scene. Drug abuse remained a part of his life until his death. In 1965, the band changed its name to The Grateful Dead and over the next three decades devoted itself to psychedelic rock, with ever-more-complex music and lyrics.

Though the band had a successful recording career, it was the live concerts that drew a hard-core near-cult-level following, some of whom, called Deadheads, would tag after the group from show to show, becoming a sideshow and cultural phenomenon of their own.

Garcia even made a solo album in 1971 and another album a year later, in which he played every instrument but drums. The group starred in a documentary film and continued to increase in popularity and expand its musical horizons. It survived various members' deaths but not Garcia's, disbanding at the end of 1995.

ANTONIO CARLOS JOBIM
Composer, Musician
(1927–1994)

Born in Rio de Janeiro in 1927, Antonio Carlos Jobim was one of the primary creators of the bossa nova musical form, which became such a big hit in the United States in the sixties, when Stan Getz and Charlie Byrd recorded the songs with their blend of traditional Brazilian samba rhythms and American jazz.

Jobim began studying music and improvising while he was still a child, and as a teenager he took more formal training in composition. He scrapped plans to become an architect and turned to music, inspired by American bandleaders performing in Rio.

He worked for a Brazilian recording company and his music gained local popularity in the fifties. International attention came when he wrote the music for *Black Orpheus*, a play that was turned into a French-Brazilian film that won an Oscar and a Cannes award in 1959.

Jobim, who periodically had lived and worked in Los Angeles, eventually emigrated to America to find more privacy and a more settled political and economic climate than he had in Brazil. "The Girl from Ipanema" is one of his most popular songs; others reflect his concern for the environment. He has given concerts all over the United States, playing the piano, even singing and dancing.

He received the Organization of American States' Diplôme de Honneur for "exceptional talents and outstanding work on behalf of music in the Americas" and has been inducted into the Songwriters Hall of Fame. He also wrote film scores and commercial jingles.

VINCENT LOPEZ
Bandleader, Pianist
(1895–1975)

Vincent Lopez was born in 1895 in Brooklyn, New York, to parents of Portuguese descent. He had a strict upbringing and his father, a bandmaster and music teacher as well as a jeweler, included several hours a day at the piano as part of his son's regimen. His father wanted his son to be a priest, but after three years in a monastery Lopez left. His disappointed father sent him to business college instead, and Lopez did work for a while as secretary to an executive, but he would play piano at nights in Clayton's, a Brooklyn saloon.

Fired from one saloon job because he wouldn't drink beer or hard liquor, Lopez continued to pursue his career. Once, he had to substitute for a bandleader, and when that man left, Lopez became the youngest orchestra leader in New York. He played for vaudeville and musical comedies along the way but really hit his stride when he landed his first hotel bandleader job at the Hotel Pennsylvania. That led to radio appearances, jazz concerts, and tours. He and his band played for President Coolidge's inauguration. He introduced jazz in London, opened his own nightclub, which burned down, and he worked at the St. Regis. He was most famous for his decades-long stint at the Hotel Taft.

He worked on television in that medium's early days, and developed a lot of big-name talent—from Rudy Vallee and the Dorsey brothers to Glenn Miller and Artie Shaw—and even gained some fame as a numerologist. Lopez lectured about music to college students, experimented with the effect of swing music on mental patients, and wrote a few books to round out his varied career.

THE NEW WORLD

THE ISLANDS: CUBA AND PUERTO RICO

LOUIS AGASSIZ FUERTES
Master Illustrator
(1874–1927)

By the age of fifteen, Louis Fuertes had already decided to spend his life studying and drawing birds. Having seen a copy of John Audubon's *Birds of America*, Fuertes was inspired at an early age.

Fuertes spent most of his life in Ithaca, New York, where his father, Estevan Antonio Fuertes, taught at Cornell University. After graduating from college, Fuertes continued to study ornithology. He traveled extensively to increase his knowledge of birds, visiting not only the United States but Canada, Mexico, and South America. He was included in the famous 1899 Harriman Expedition, which went to Alaska to conduct scientific research.

In 1923, Fuertes became a lecturer in ornithology at Cornell. His illustrations grace the pages of the leading bird books published between 1896 and 1927.

In 1927, at the age of fifty-three, Fuertes was tragically killed at a rail-crossing accident in Ithaca. At the memorial service at Cornell University, his longtime friend Dr. Frank Chapman said that "if the birds of the world had met to select a human being who could best express to mankind the beauty of their rhythmic flight, their manners for the heart's delight, they would unquestionably have chosen Louis Fuertes."

OSCAR HIJUELOS
Novelist
(1951–   )

Born in New York City in 1951 to parents who had emigrated from Cuba in the previous decade, not for political but economic reasons, Oscar Hijuelos has lived most of his life in that city's Spanish Harlem and spoke Spanish before he learned English.

Although he tried a variety of jobs after high school, including a stint as a farmer in Wisconsin, Hijuelos became interested in writing and returned to New York. He enrolled in City College of New York, where he earned a bachelor's and a master's degree, then set out to write short stories and novels.

The Latin flavor of his first novel, *Our House in the Lost World*, won him not only critical praise but the Rome Prize for Literature, which meant a year of free living in Rome, and he headed for Italy to start on his second novel. He would tap the nostalgia for Cuba he had heard expressed during his childhood, the reminiscences of an uncle who had been a musician with Desi Arnaz and Xavier Cugat in Havana, and the growing popularity of Latin music in the United States.

That novel, *The Mambo Kings Play Songs of Love*, recounts the story of two Cuban musicians who come to New York during the fifties, manage to fulfill their dream of appearing on the *I Love Lucy* TV show, win some fame, but eventually slide downhill to tragedy.

It won for Hijuelos the Pulitzer Prize for Fiction, a Guggenheim fellowship, and the Ingram Merrill Foundation Award.

NICHOLASA
MOHR
Author, Illustrator
(1935–   )

Born November 1, 1935, in New York City, Nicholasa Mohr was raised in a Spanish neighborhood by her Puerto Rican parents, Pedro and Nicholasa Rivera Golpe.

Mohr utilized her skill and talent as an illustrator long before becoming an author of young adult books. Prior to becoming a novelist, she was a well-known printmaker for almost eighteen years. For this career, she studied and worked her way through various art schools, including Brooklyn Museum Art School, the Arts Students League, and the Pratt Center for Contemporary Printmaking.

Her first novel, *Nilda,* was an immediate success, winning the Jane Addams Children's Book Award for 1974 and being included in the *School Library Journal*'s Best of the Best 1966–1978 list. Mohr designed the book jacket herself and received the Society of Illustrators Citation of Merit. *Nilda* tells the bleak story of a young Puerto Rican girl's impoverished youth and what it was like growing up as a member of a scorned minority.

Nilda was soon followed by *El Bronx Remembered, In Nueva York,* and *Felita.* They have been named notable trade books in the field of social studies by the joint committee of the National Council for the Social Studies and the Children's Book Council. Mohr also contributes short stories to *Children's Digest, Scholastic* magazine, and *Nuestro.* She has also written for public television and radio. She is currently at work on a novel and has received an honorary doctorate from the State University of New York at Albany.

There have been too many Hispanic boxing champions and contenders throughout the past four decades to feature in even four books this size, but several deserve mention here.

WILFREDO BENITEZ

World Champion Boxer (1958–)

Benitez was born September 12, 1958, in Puerto Rico. On March 6, 1976, he became the youngest boxer to win a world boxing championship. The seventeen-and-a-half-year-old won the WBA Light-Welterweight title in San Juan, Puerto Rico. He went on to capture world titles in three different weight classes, a feat that only a handful of fighters have accomplished in the long history of professional boxing.

CARLOS ORTIZ

World Champion Boxer (1936–)

Ortiz was born September 9, 1936, in Ponce, Puerto Rico. He became a pro in 1955, winning the vacant World Junior Welterweight Title in 1959, and in 1962, he won the World Lightweight Title. His long career in the ring came to an end in 1972. Ortiz was awarded the Edward J. Neil Trophy and entered the Boxing Hall of Fame in 1988.

Other Hispanic professional boxers to be selected for the Boxing Hall of Fame:

Sixto Escobar, 1975
Ceferino Garcia, 1977
Daniel Mendoza, 1954
Jose Napoles, 1985 . . . 1969 *Ring* magazine "Fighter of the Year"
Manuel Ortiz, 1985
Pascual Perez, 1977
Pancho Villa, 1961

JOSE CANSECO
Baseball Player
(1964–   )

Jose Canseco, Jr., was born July 2, 1964, in Regla, Cuba. The Canseco family, one of the most prominent in the Havana area prior to the Communist revolution, struggled for several years following the Castro takeover, when Canseco's father lost his job and his home. In December 1965, Jose, Sr., with less than fifty dollars in his pocket, was allowed to leave Cuba and take his family to the Miami area.

Canseco's parents stressed academic excellence, and although he did play soccer and basketball as a child, he did not pick up a baseball until he was thirteen. Although he tried out every year, he did not make his high school varsity baseball team until his senior year.

On the advice of a scout, the Oakland A's selected Canseco in the fifteenth round of the 1982 draft. After playing for several years in the minor leagues, Jose made his major-league debut with the A's on September 2, 1985.

During the next few years, Canseco continually posted the statistics of a top power hitter. In 1988, he became the first player in history to hit 40 home runs and steal 40 bases in the same season. Finishing the season with a batting average of .307, 124 RBIs, 42 home runs, and 40 stolen bases, he was unanimously selected as the American League's MVP.

In 1990, Canseco signed a five-year contract for $23.5 million, making him baseball's highest-paid player at that time. That year he was the leading vote-getter among the fans' ballots for the All-Star game. He was later traded to the Texas Rangers.

Canseco currently plays for the Boston Red Sox. He enjoys doing charity work for organizations that help children, including the Make-a-Wish Foundation.

ROBERTO WALKER CLEMENTE
Baseball Star
(1934–1972)

As a child in Carolina, Puerto Rico, Roberto Clemente, the son of a sugarcane worker, once made his own baseball because he was too poor to buy one. Although small and thin in his early years, by 1954 when scouts from the Brooklyn Dodgers came to Puerto Rico looking for new talent, Clemente had become an excellent ballplayer. Scout Al Campanis later commented, "He was the greatest natural athlete I have ever seen. . . ." Clemente signed with the Dodgers and played for their farm team in Montreal. He was the first-draft pick of the Pittsburgh Pirates in 1954.

Clemente was a popular player in Pittsburgh where he played a major role in their winning the 1960 and 1971 World Series. Despite all types of injuries and illnesses, he played eighteen seasons as a Pirate, winning four National League batting championships and playing on twelve All-Star teams, and joined the ranks of the elite by getting his 3,000th hit in 1972. His lifetime batting average was .313.

In December 1972, Clemente was moved by the plight of those devastated by an earthquake in Nicaragua. He solicited food and medicine from his friends and agreed to accompany the goods on the flight to Managua. The heavily laden cargo plane crashed shortly after takeoff. His body was never found. The governor of Puerto Rico ordered three days of national mourning for Puerto Rico's beloved athlete.

Voting overwhelmingly to set aside the five-year eligibility rule, the Baseball Writers' Association elected Clemente to Baseball's Hall of Fame less than three months after his death.

ANGEL CORDERO
Jockey, Trainer
(1942–   )

Born in Santurce, Puerto Rico, on May 8, 1942, Angel Tomás Cordero, Jr., was literally destined for a career in horse racing. His father was a horse trainer and former jockey; both of his grandfathers and a score of uncles and cousins also had been professional jockeys.

Although he had been on the back of a horse since infancy and had been trained in the techniques necessary for being a jockey from age three, his mother at first resisted his desires to become one. But he was off to the races at age eighteen, starting at El Commandante, San Juan's racetrack. After two successful years there, he headed for the major New York tracks.

There he met with frustration. He was unknown, could speak little English, and had no contracts. He returned to race in Puerto Rico but in 1965 took a second shot at New York, determined to stick it out. In 1968, he was the leading jockey in victories in the United States, and he remained a major force in the saddle for decades. Once he set a New York record by winning five consecutive races in one day, adding a sixth win later that day.

At 5'3", Cordero had no trouble with weight. Strong and wiry, he proved to be a skillful and courageous rider. His aggressive riding style brought him many suspensions but also many victories. In 1974, he and Lafitt Pincay became the first two jockeys in history whose mounts earned more than $4 million in a single year. Cordero retired as a jockey in 1992 and now trains racehorses. He, his wife, and their two children live the affluent lifestyle in Long Island that his success has earned. He remains a hero among Puerto Ricans.

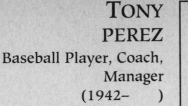

TONY
PEREZ
Baseball Player, Coach, Manager
(1942–   )

Atanasio Rigal Perez was born in Camaquey, Cuba, May 14, 1942. The 6'2" Perez spent the first seventeen years of his pro career in the Cincinnati Reds organization. He began his career in 1960 playing for Geneva of the New York–Penn League as a seventeen-year-old. A year later, he led that league with a .348 average. He was the Pacific Coast League's MVP in 1964 for San Diego, ending that season in a Reds uniform, which he was to wear for the next twelve seasons. From 1967 to 1976, Perez had more RBIs (1,028) than any other player in major-league baseball, even though he never won an RBI championship.

In 1970, he had his best overall season, when he batted .317 with 40 homers and 129 RBIs. Perez played in six Championship Series and five World Series. He appeared in seven All-Star games and was MVP of the 1967 game at Anaheim, hitting a fifteenth-inning game-winning homer off Catfish Hunter.

A first baseman throughout most of his career, Perez was the first player ever to hit a homer into the red seats at Riverfront Stadium (August 11, 1970, off Met Jim McAndrew). An integral part of the "Big Red Machine" of the 1970s, Perez broke an 0-for-15 slump in the 1975 World Series vs. Boston by belting two homers and driving in four runs in Cincinnati's Game 5 victory. He homered off Bill Lee in Game 7 to help the Reds come from behind and beat the Red Sox, 4–3. In 1985, one day short of his forty-third birthday, Perez became the oldest player ever to hit a bases-loaded homer in the majors. He put the perfect cap on his twenty-three-year major-league career when he hit his 379th home run on October 4, 1986, one day before his retirement as a player. Perez managed the Reds from 1992 to 1994, after six years on the team's coaching staff.

CHI CHI RODRIGUEZ
PGA Golf Pro
(1935–   )

The 5'7", 132-pound, high-spirited, quick-swinging Chi Chi Rodriguez was born in Bayamón, Puerto Rico, on October 23, 1935. As a youngster, he worked his way into the game of golf by hitting tin cans with a guava-tree stick. As a professional, he joined the Professional Golf Association Tour in 1960.

Rodriguez won his first PGA tournament, the Denver Open, in 1963. His last PGA Tour victory was the Tallahassee Open in 1979, which gave him a total of eight major tour victories, with a total career PGA Tour earnings of $1,037,105.

In 1985, he joined the Senior PGA Tour, becoming a tougher competitor, and claiming more than twenty tour victories and earnings reaching $3,740,267 (as of 1992).

In his first year on the Senior Tour, he didn't win more than one event, but still managed consistency with seventeen top ten finishes, including five runner-up spots. He finished among the top five on the money list, winning the Ko Olina at the end of the year by six strokes, and setting a new course record.

In 1990, Rodriguez won four tournaments in seven weeks early in the season. He started his run by winning with a pair of 66s at the rain-shortened GTE West Classic. In 1991, he became the only winner of back-to-back events on the senior circuit when he beat Jim Colbert in a four-hole play-off while defending his Las Vegas crown. In the Silver Pages Classic, he set a Senior Tour record with eight straight birdies.

Rodriguez donates much of what he wins to needy children through his foundation. One fund-raiser is his "Chi Chi and the Bear" golf outing with Jack Nicklaus, which so far has reaped $1 million. One of his many awards is the Bob Jones Award, the United States Golf Association's highest honor.

Eduardo Aguirre, Jr.

Banking Executive
(1946–   )

Born in Cuba on July 30, 1946, and a U.S. citizen, Eduardo Aguirre is a nationally recognized Hispanic business leader. In 1990, 1991, and 1992, Mr. Aguirre was named one of the hundred most influential Hispanics in the nation by *Hispanic Business Magazine*.

Mr. Aguirre has been in banking for twenty-six years and is NationsBank's international private banking executive, with activities in Houston, Dallas, San Antonio, Atlanta, and Miami. NationsBank is the fourth-largest banking organization in the United States.

Mr. Aguirre is a prominent Hispanic community leader and has a long history of public service. He has been appointed by President Bush to the National Commission for Employment Policy, and by the Supreme Court of Texas to the state bar as a non-attorney director.

A graduate of LSU and of the National Commercial Lending Graduate School, Mr. Aguirre is a certified commercial lender and has completed studies at several international banking schools. He is former co-chairman of the Hispanic-Jewish Business Round Table of the Anti-Defamation League, and is president of the Hispanic Political Action Committee. He is a board member of St. Joseph Hospital and of the Houston chapter of the American Red Cross.

Mr. Aguirre and his wife, Tere, have lived in Houston since 1975 with their two children, Eddy and Tessie.

MARIA ELENA ALVAREZ
Sales Executive
(1947–   )

Alvarez was born in Havana, Cuba, July 11, 1947. She left her native Cuba at age thirteen under Operation Peter Pan, a program to relocate Cuban children in the United States, away from Marxist indoctrination. Today, she is a resident of Guaynabo, Puerto Rico.

Alvarez attended Worth Business College in 1966. Later, she enrolled at the University of Puerto Rico, majoring in marketing and public relations. From 1970 to 1972, she was Partido Nuevo Progresista campaign coordinator.

She joined Mary Kay Cosmetics in 1975; one year later, she was named director of sales in Puerto Rico. "I have achieved many of my dreams," she says, "especially having a career that allows me to spend more time with my family and children."

In the fall of 1992, Maria Elena Alvarez was named national sales director of Mary Kay Cosmetics, the first Hispanic to reach that position. Alvarez has a mission besides selling cosmetics: "I want to help break the barriers for Hispanic women by teaching them to believe in themselves and realize that they, too, can gain success."

She's the first Hispanic in Mary Kay to have earned over one million dollars in commissions.

LUIS A. FERRE
Industrialist, Politician
(1904–   )

Born in Ponce, Puerto Rico, in 1904, Luis A. Ferre's education included degrees in mechanical and electrical engineering from MIT, as he prepared for a role in his engineer father's business, Ferre Industries.

When the United States needed a naval base in Puerto Rico during World War II, the Ferre firm was given a loan to start the Ponce Cement Company to assist in the project. In 1950, the Puerto Rican government gave the family money-losing paper, glass, and clay plants, which they turned into money-makers. The Ferres also bought stock in a Florida company and took it over in 1954, then played a major role in the building of Miami Beach hotels.

Politically, Luis Ferre was aligned with the Republican Statehood Party, headed by a relative. It favored statehood for Puerto Rico rather than the commonwealth status supported by long-time Governor Luis Muñoz Marín and his Popular Democratic Party. Ferre won an at-large seat in Puerto Rico's legislature in 1956, ran unsuccessfully against Muñoz Marín for governor several times, but then became governor in 1968, winning on a platform of farm wage subsidization, slum rehabilitation, a war on narcotics, and a go-slow approach on statehood.

Ferre Industries has prospered and Ponce has benefited through gifts of a university, art museum, and library. Luis plays classical piano and reads French literature. Among his many honors are being named a Knight of the Holy Sepulchre by Pope John and being cited as exemplary of Puerto Rican ambitions by a youth agency.

ROBERT C. GOIZUETA

Chairman of the Board and
Chief Executive Officer,
the Coca-Cola Company
(1931–   )

Mr. Goizueta was born in Havana, Cuba, on November 18, 1931. He was educated in Havana and later attended Yale University, where he received his B.S. degree in chemical engineering in 1953.

Mr. Goizueta has been associated with Coca-Cola since 1954, when he was employed by the technical department of a subsidiary of the Coca-Cola Company, Cia. Embotelladora Coca-Cola, S.A., in Havana. In 1961 he was transferred to Nassau as area chemist in the Caribbean Area Office of the Coca-Cola Export Corporation and in 1963 he was named staff assistant to the senior vice president for Latin America.

In 1964, Mr. Goizueta was transferred to company headquarters in Atlanta, and a year later he was named assistant to the vice president, Technical Research and Development. In 1966, he was elected vice president. His election to senior vice president, Technical Division, followed in 1974, and his election to executive vice president came in May 1975. Mr. Goizueta was elected vice chairman of the company in 1979. In May 1980 Mr. Goizueta was elected president and CEO and a director of the company. He became chairman of the board and chief executive officer on March 1, 1981.

Mr. Goizueta is a director of Trust Company of Georgia, Sun-Trust Banks, SONAT, the Ford Motor Company, and Eastman Kodak Company. His numerous civic awards and his service to the community reflect Mr. Goizueta's merits.

Mr. Goizueta lives in Atlanta, Georgia, with his wife, the former Olga Casteleiro, and their three children, Roberto, Olga Maria (Mrs. Thompson T. Rawls II), and Javier.

JUAN GUITERAS
Medical Researcher
(1852–1925)

Born in Matanzas, Cuba, in 1852, Juan Guiteras left with his family when they were forced to depart in 1868 for political reasons. They came to the United States, where he went to the University of Pennsylvania, graduating from its medical school, practicing at the university hospital, and teaching his speciality, tropical diseases. He later joined the staff of the Marine Hospital Service in Washington, D.C.

Yellow fever, a deadly tropical disease, became a special interest of his, and he spent much of the late nineteenth century touring hospitals in Cuba and the West Indies, seeking answers to the mysteries of that disease. Dr. Guiteras research led him to a breakthrough theory: that children living in areas where the disease struck could develop immunity through very mild bouts of the fever contracted during childhood. He also supported the theories of another Cuban, Dr. Carlos Finlay, who laid blame for spread of the disease on the mosquito. They noted that cities high above sea level, where mosquitoes could not breed, tended not to have the disease.

Early in the twentieth century, a medical team led by Walter Reed proved these theories correct. If mosquito breeding grounds were eliminated, the disease could be prevented.

Dr. Guiteras, a Rockefeller Foundation consultant on yellow fever, lived the final years of his life in Cuba, teaching pathology and tropical diseases at the University of Havana and becoming Cuba's first director of public health.

ORESTES LORENZO
Pilot of Courage
(1956–   )

For almost two years after arriving in Florida, Lorenzo, an ex-Cuban MIG-23 fighter pilot, planned constantly on somehow returning to his homeland and rescuing his loving family.

For months he tried to win his family's release through publicizing their plight. He had the support of the Valladares Foundation and of Human Rights, both Washington-based human rights groups headed by Cuban-Americans. He even passed out leaflets bearing his family's picture during anti-Castro demonstrations. Later, he spoke passionately to members of the UN Human Rights Commission in Geneva about his separation from his family. He left leaflets in the chairs of delegates from Cuba.

That human rights organization and other groups had postcards and balloons made up with pictures of Lorenzo's family on them, asking the world for help in reuniting him with his family. Lorenzo even visited Madrid, Spain, chaining himself to a park fence and staging a weeklong hunger strike while Castro was visiting that country.

After a personal plea from President Bush failed, Lorenzo took matters into his own hands. Elena Diaz-Verson Amos donated money to the Valladares Foundation to buy a 1961 Cessna aircraft. A week before Christmas Day 1992, Lorenzo took off for Cuba without any U.S. government support. Flying low to evade Cuban radar, he landed his small white plane on a busy highway east of Havana, rescued his wife and two small sons, and escaped to Miami and freedom.

ANTONIA NOVELLO

Surgeon General of the
United States
(1944–   )

Antonia Novello was plagued by illness throughout her childhood and teen years in Puerto Rico. She tells of being hospitalized at least two weeks each summer due to a congenital abnormality, and finally having corrective surgery when a young adult. The ordeal left her with a determination to help others by becoming a physician.

Novello graduated in 1965 from the University of Puerto Rico, and continued on for a medical degree in 1970. In that same year she married Joseph Novello, a navy flight surgeon who later became a psychiatrist. In 1976, Novello began her own private pediatric practice in Virginia, leaving it to join the U.S. Public Health Service in 1978 as a project leader at the National Institutes of Health (NIH).

Novello progressed rapidly through the ranks at NIH, and in 1986 she was named deputy director of the National Institute of Child Health and Human Development. In October 1989, President George Bush nominated her to be surgeon general. On March 9, 1990, Novello was sworn in as the fourteenth surgeon general of the United States, the first woman, first Hispanic, and first Puerto Rican to be appointed to that position. She made headlines in her role as surgeon general by her attacks on the tobacco and the liquor industries and her fight against inadequate Hispanic health care. After leaving office, she returned to Georgetown University School of Medicine in Washington, D.C., as clinical professor of Pediatrics.

Mrs. Novello resides in the Georgetown section of Washington, D.C., with her husband. She is the author of more than seventy-five articles and chapters of books dealing with pediatrics, nephrology, and public health policy.

ADMIRAL HORACIO RIVERO
Military Leader
(1910–   )

Horacio Rivero was born in Ponce, Puerto Rico, on May 16, 1910. Rivero graduated from Central High School in San Juan and entered the United States Naval Academy, Annapolis, Maryland, on an appointment from Puerto Rico on June 20, 1927. He graduated with distinction, third in a class of 441. In 1940, Rivero received his Master of Science degree in electrical engineering from MIT. This prepared him for his role as a senior gunnery officer on the warship *San Juan* during World War II.

It was during a tour in the Pacific that Admiral Rivero received the Bronze Star for his leadership in controlling gun batteries on the USS *San Juan* in support of the landing of marines on Guadalcanal on August 7, 1942, and his crew's downing several Japanese torpedo planes during the following day.

Horacio Rivero held various positions at the Pentagon after the war and was promoted several times. He was made rear admiral in 1955 after serving as assistant chief of staff for the Pacific Fleet. In 1964, he became vice chief of naval operations, and four years later he was made commander-in-chief of all Allied forces in Southern Europe.

After retiring in 1972, he was appointed United States ambassador to Spain, becoming the first Hispanic to fill that position.

LORETA JANETA VELAZQUEZ
Confederate Soldier

There are few stories as strange or exciting as that of Loreta Velazquez, born in Havana, Cuba, of aristocratic Spanish parents. In her book *The Woman in Battle*, published in 1876, Velazquez claims to have fought in the Confederate Army, disguised as a man, and using the name Lieutenant Harry T. Buford.

Velazquez and her husband, a career officer in the U.S. Army, were stationed at Fort Leavenworth, Kansas, when the Civil War began. Velazquez became a fierce supporter of the Confederacy and persuaded her husband to leave the U.S. Army and fight for the South. It was shortly thereafter that Velazquez began her masquerade. Supposedly she fought at the First Battle of Bull Run in 1861, at Fort Donelson, and again at the Battle of Shiloh in 1862. She claims to have been wounded at the latter two battles, which ended her army career, but not her fight for the Confederacy. She continued to act as a spy and blockade runner.

Though there may be some element of truth to her story, there is little to substantiate it. In fact, one of her most vocal critics was ex–Confederate General Jubal A. Early. The life of Loreta Janeta Velazquez is a strange mix of fact and fantasy.

DESI
ARNAZ
Actor, Musician, TV Producer
(1917–1986)

Desiderio Alberto Arnaz y de Acha III was born in Santiago, Cuba, March 2, 1917, to a family of very wealthy landowners. His father was mayor of Santiago, Cuba, but this all ended with a Cuban revolution in August 1933. They lost all their wealth and his father was imprisoned. Soon after, his family came to the United States. As a seventeen-year-old, Arnaz eked out a living driving trucks and cabs.

In 1934, he caught the eye of bandleader Xavier Cugat while performing in Miami. After a short stint with the Cugat band, Arnaz formed his own and created the conga music craze of the 1930s. His big break came in 1939, when he starred in the Broadway hit musical *Too Many Girls*, by Rodgers and Hart. Later, the movie version paired Arnaz with a new actress named Lucille Ball. They were married in 1940 and worked on their solo careers.

Upon joining the U.S. Army as a new American citizen, he was advised by the recruiter to shorten his extra-long name— hence, Desi Arnaz.

In 1950 he and Lucille created Desilu Productions and produced such hit television shows as *The Danny Thomas Show*, *The Untouchables*, *Our Miss Brooks*, and of course *I Love Lucy*, which lasted from 1951 to 1961 and was the first television show in history to reach 10 million homes. The hectic schedule of Desilu's many productions strained their marriage, and in 1960 Lucille and Desi were divorced.

Arnaz sold his share of Desilu to Lucille in 1962 and retired to his horse ranch in Del Mar, California, where he died in 1986 at the age of sixty-nine.

HECTOR ELIZONDO
Actor
(1936–   )

Born in New York City in 1936 to parents who had been raised in Puerto Rico, Hector Elizondo grew up in an ethnically and racially mixed neighborhood near Harlem. That background has served him well as a popular character actor who has portrayed a wide array of roles.

He was interested in music as a child and the noted blues composer W. C. Handy praised his voice and recommended him for the Frank Murray Boys Choir, with whom he appeared on radio and television. He even became a voice major at New York's High School of Music and Art. After a year at City College of New York, during which he played guitar and conga drums with a band, Elizondo quit school to earn money for his wife and young child.

He played for rehearsals of a ballet company and once, after walking through a yet uncast part, won the role plus an offer to study dance. A knee injury canceled a chance to be in a national tour of *West Side Story*. When a director whom Elizondo helped lose weight at the health club where he worked gave him an acting job, he decided to stick with that career.

After a number of plays, which led to major roles in *The Great White Hope* and *Steambath*, he resisted typecasting as a Hispanic performer and held out for such roles as the lead in *The Prisoner of Second Avenue*. On television, he made a number of dramatic appearances and starred in two short-lived sitcoms. In film, *The Taking of Pelham One Two Three* and *Pretty Woman* were major efforts that won him critical attention. He currently stars in the television hospital drama *Chicago Hope*.

GLORIA ESTEFAN
Singer, Composer, Dancer
(1958–   )

Born in Havana, Cuba, in 1958, Gloria Estefan was taken to Miami by her parents a year later after Fidel Castro assumed power. Her father, a policeman who had guarded dictator Fulgencio Batista's wife, later took part in the ill-fated Bay of Pigs invasion of his homeland and was imprisoned. He was later disabled in the Vietnam War.

Estefan attended a Catholic high school and began to sing and play the guitar. She went on to study psychology and communications at the University of Miami, worked for the Department of Immigration as a translator, and taught guitar.

In 1974, she joined the Miami Latin Boys, a group led by Emilio Estefan, who took a risk adding a female to the traditional all-male group, which toured Mexico and Central and South America. The two eventually married. The group was renamed the Miami Sound Machine, with Estefan as lead singer and occasional composer, and it enjoyed success in concerts, recordings, and even films leading to her eventual success as a solo act.

In 1990, the same year she was invited to the White House to discuss an antidrug campaign with President Bush, Estefan hosted the American Music Awards. Soon afterward, the group's tour bus was involved in a severe accident during a snowstorm in New York State. Her back was broken. Thousands of fans sent cards and flowers as she mended in a hospital and then underwent nearly a year of tedious and painful therapy. She resumed her singing/composing/dancing career with an appearance at the American Music Awards in 1991. Estefan was named the Humanitarian of the Year by B'nai B'rith in 1992 and the Musicians Person of the Year in 1994 for her charitable efforts. She has had over seventeen Top Ten Hits and has sold over 20 million copies of her albums.

JOSE FELICIANO
Singer, Guitarist
(1945–   )

Blind when born in Lárez, Puerto Rico, in 1945, Jose Feliciano had to struggle against his handicap, family poverty, and prejudice to find his place in life. When it became too difficult to eke out a living on their farm, his parents moved to New York City in 1950.

Young Feliciano would listen to the radio, imitate the voices he heard, and enjoy the music. He was determined to go into that field. He was given a guitar when he was nine and performed publicly for the first time that year at El Teatro Puerto Rico in New York. He continued to appear at talent shows and school assemblies. His early musical influences were Elvis Presley, Fats Domino, Chuck Berry, Ray Charles, and Sam Cooke.

Blocked from many normal teen pursuits, Feliciano went to coffeehouses in Greenwich Village, seeking opportunities to perform for the coins people would give him. He began adding humorous banter about his blindness to relax audiences. At seventeen, he dropped out of school to do a gig in a Detroit nightclub. An RCA talent scout heard him at a New York performance and signed him to a recording contract. Not sure what musical style he would adopt, Feliciano moved to California, tapped his Latin roots, and began hitting the charts. "Light My Fire" became a major hit for him and opened the door to such big-time showcases as Las Vegas. He remains a popular recording star outside the United States, earning gold and platinum albums in 1993.

JOSE FERRER

Actor, Director
(1912–1992)

Born in Santurce, Puerto Rico, in 1912, Jose Vincente Ferrer de Otero y Cintron came to the United States as a child and studied architecture at Princeton University. But the stage was his first love, and he became a major figure on Broadway, in films, and on TV. He had a rich, easily recognized voice and had the ability to play farce as well as drama and everything in between.

Ferrer's memberships included the Academy of Arts and Sciences of Puerto Rico and the Screen Actors Guild. He is in the Theatre Hall of Fame, was named ambassador of the arts by the State of Florida, and served as artistic adviser to the Coconut Grove Playhouse. He won Tony Awards for both acting and directing on Broadway. He also won Oscar and Emmy statuettes.

On the stage he played in such varied productions as *Othello*, *Stalag 17*, *The Fourposter*, *My Three Angels*, *Cyrano de Bergerac*, and *Charley's Aunt*. His films include *The Caine Mutiny*, *Moulin Rouge*, *The Shrike*, *Lawrence of Arabia*, and *Ship of Fools*. On TV, he acted in *A Case of Libel*, *What Makes Sammy Run*, *The Rhinemann Exchange*, a host of video films, and guest appearances on such series as *Quincy* and *Newhart*. He also produced and wrote scripts.

His special honors include the American Academy of Arts and Sciences Gold Medal, the National Medal of the Arts, and the Hispanic Heritage Festival Don Quixote Award. Two of his wives have been celebrities: actress Uta Hagen and singer Rosemary Clooney.

RAÚL JULIA
Actor
(1940–1994)

San Juan native Raúl Rafael Carlos Julia y Arcelay had a restaurateur father and homemaker mother who saw to it that their son attended the University of Puerto Rico, where he earned a B.A.

He came to New York at age twenty-two to seek acting jobs, but had difficulty breaking into mainstream productions. However, he did find work and training in Hispanic theaters there. His talent was not to be denied. Producer Joseph Papp saw his potential and hired him for his New York Shakespeare Festival, where Julia's work in *Two Gentlemen of Verona* in 1971 won him the first of four Tony Award nominations.

His versatility as an actor, as well as the force of his personality, could be seen in the range of successes that came his way thereafter. On television, he portrayed Rafael, the Fixit Man, on *Sesame Street*, Aristotle Onassis in a miniseries, martyred Brazilian labor leader Chico Mendas, along with roles in an array of made-for-video films. His off-Broadway credits included *The Ox Cart* and *No Exit*. He appeared on Broadway in *Man of La Mancha*, *Threepenny Opera*, *The Cuban Thing*, and *Where's Charley?*

Julia's big-screen movie career was capped by his powerful performance in *Kiss of the Spider Woman*, but his roles also encompassed lighter fare—Gomez in the Addams Family films, for example—as well as thrillers such as *The Eyes of Laura Mars* and *The Plague*.

RITA MORENO

Actress, Dancer, Singer
(1931–   )

Born in Humacao near Puerto Rico's rain forest in 1931, Rosa Dolores Alverio began at an early age to train for a show-business career that would bring a unique honor: a spot in the *Guinness Book of Records* as the only performer ever to win all four major entertainment awards.

At age five, she was brought to New York by her recently divorced mother, took dancing lessons, and soon began performing in Macy's toy department children's theater and at various functions. She sang and danced her way through the teen years in small nightclubs and in a show that died quickly on Broadway. She often dubbed child-star dialogue in movies headed for Spanish-speaking countries.

She did bits in films and was signed to an MGM contract under the name of Rosita Moreno, the surname being her stepfather's. Soon the first name became Rita. MGM dropped her and she freelanced in Hollywood but was upset by the stereotypical roles she received. She eventually returned to a career that shifted constantly from film to theater to nightclubs to television.

Persistence and talent paid off. The awards that got her into the record books: a supporting actress Oscar for *West Side Story*; a Tony for a Broadway comedy role in *The Ritz*; a Grammy for the soundtrack album of her children's television series, *The Electric Company*; and two Emmy awards for guest appearances on *The Muppet Show* and *The Rockford Files*. In 1990, Moreno won the Hispanic Heritage Award in the performing arts. She continues to work in the theater, most recently pairing with her daughter in *Steel Magnolias*.

SALLY JESSY
RAPHAEL
Radio, TV Personality
(1943–   )

Born into a prosperous family in 1943 in Easton, Pennsylvania, Sally Jessy Raphael enjoyed an affluent childhood. After a stay in San Juan, Puerto Rico, her family moved back to the States where her father's continuing illness drained the family fortunes. She yearned for a career in radio and got a job reading school news on the air, took broadcasting courses at Columbia University, and even studied at the famous Actor's Studio in New York.

After an early marriage, she returned to San Juan, where she gave birth to two children and her broadcasting career. Her jobs ranged from news to weather, from a talk show and cooking show to serving as AP correspondent. Raphael was divorced, then married a San Juan radio executive who had encouraged her. They moved to Miami, where she did a late-night talk show but left in a long search nationwide for a better job. From rock-and-roll disc jockey to television puppet show hostess, Sally Jessy, who as a youngster had added her mother's maiden name, Raphael, kept busy trying to establish herself.

Back in Miami, she anchored a morning TV show and an afternoon radio interview show. In 1976, she cohosted a New York talk show with Barry Farber. Earning a trial on a new night-time radio call-in show, she clicked in the format and her career took off. She was chosen for a television version in 1983. Six years later, a syndicated version won her the Daytime Emmy Award for outstanding talk show host and, in 1990, an Emmy for best talk show.

CHITA RIVERA

Actress, Dancer, Singer
(1933–   )

Born in Washington, D.C., in 1933 to Puerto Rican parents, Dolores Conchita Figuero del Rivero got some early show-business experience performing in shows at home arranged by her older brother. She attended an array of singing, piano, and ballet classes, winning a prestigious scholarship to the Balanchine School of American Ballet in New York City.

She appeared as a dancer in the national touring company of *Call Me Madam* in 1952 and then went into *Guys and Dolls* and *Can-Can*. She was encouraged to broaden her performing skills by *Can-Can* star Gwen Verdon and appeared in the off-Broadway *Shoestring Revue*. She won praise for a role in the Sammy Davis Jr. show, *Mr. Wonderful*, then appeared in *West Side Story* and *Bye Bye Birdie*, roles which won her Tony nominations.

Chita Rivera has performed in cabarets, on many TV musical shows, and with national touring company shows such as *Zorba, Kiss Me Kate*, and *Sweet Charity*. She played a lesser role in the film version of *Charity* but did not enjoy the Hollywood experience. The stage is her first love, and she has racked up some dramatic efforts. Triumphs in that medium for Chita Rivera include *Chicago* and *The Rink*.

She has won Tony awards for best actress in a musical for her roles in *The Rink* and *Kiss of the Spider Woman*.

ENTERTAINERS

GERALDO RIVERA
TV Talk Show Host
(1943–)

Born in New York City in 1943 to an immigrant Puerto Rican father and an Eastern European Jewish immigrant mother, Geraldo Miguel Rivera grew up in Brooklyn. His family moved to the Long Island community of Babylon, where he attended high school, concentrating more on sports than studies. He needed remedial English and math to be accepted into the state maritime college, after which he served in the merchant marine for two years.

He got his B.S. degree at the University of Arizona, where he felt uncomfortable because of his Hispanic and New York accent, and returned to get his law degree from Brooklyn College. He specialized in poverty law, working with neighborhood legal aid offices.

Rivera became a bilingual reporter at a New York television station, underwent training at Columbia University's Graduate School of Journalism, and joined the station's Eyewitness News Team. He began to develop the hard-nosed, aggressive style of advocacy journalism that has helped him climb out of the ranks to stardom in the medium. He covered such topics as drug addiction, migrant workers, problems of Vietnam veterans, and mistreatment by welfare institutions. He earned his station journalistic honors and became the subject of a USIA documentary aimed at Latin American audiences.

As he moved up the station and network ladder, Rivera honed these aggressive techniques. He now produces and hosts a provocative top-rated syndicated talk show, as well as appearing on CNBC.

JIMMY SMITS
Actor
(1955–   )

Born in Brooklyn, New York, in 1955, Jimmy Smits used his acting skills as the stepping-stone to a career that has earned him not only show business honors but such tributes as "King of Brooklyn," a title bestowed on prominent ex-Brooklynites who come back to inspire and help their former neighbors, and the 1987 Hispanic Media Image Task Force Imagen Award. His mother came from Puerto Rico and his father from Surinam. Life was difficult for the young Smits, but that did not discourage him.

He pursued a higher education, earning a B.A. from Brooklyn College and an M.A. from Cornell University. Indeed, in his talks with Hispanic children, Smits continues to promote education as "the key and foundation for everything."

Soap operas, considered a challenging show-business training ground, proved to be a fruitful path for Smits. He appeared in *All My Children*, *Another World*, *The Guiding Light*, and *One Life to Live*. He has worked in the theater and has made appearances on such series as *Miami Vice*, as well as in a number of made-for-video movies. When a shot came along for a major role on a new network series, Smits was ready. *L.A. Law* became a very popular hit and won for Smits a coveted Emmy Award. His most recent television success has come as a star of the highly acclaimed police drama *NYPD Blue*.

He also has tried his hand at feature films. His efforts include *Switch* and *Fires Within*.

THE NEW WORLD

MEXICO

RUDOLFO A. ANAYA
Author
(1937–   )

Rudolfo Anaya was born in Pastura, New Mexico, in 1937 and has blended his Hispanic heritage, writing skills, and education in literature into a career as educator and author. He is considered one of the major writers of Hispanic–based fiction of his generation.

Anaya attended the University of New Mexico, where he earned a bachelor's and master's degree in literature, as well as a master's degree in guidance counseling. He is a professor of English at that institution, but it is his books that have brought him such wide acclaim.

He draws his stories from the folktales of the Southwest's Mexican-Indian population and from Spanish-American legends, leavened with cultural conflicts, religious overtones, even ancient paganism, and enhanced skillfully through artful narrative techniques. He makes the personal conflicts his characters face part of an earthly manifestation of an ongoing, unseen clash between good and evil conducted on a cosmic scale. But the critics go beyond such appraisals to note that his work is far more than a mere ethnic art form and can appeal to all readers.

His first novel, *Bless Me, Ultima*, was published in 1972 and has sold nearly 300,000 copies. It earned for Anaya the Premio Quinto Sol. A subsequent novel, *Tortuga*, published in 1979, won the American Book Award of the Before Columbus Foundation. He has published nine books, along with various plays and screenplays.

CARLOS CALLEJO
Artist/Muralist
(1952–   )

Carlos Callejo was born in Ciudad Juárez, Mexico, the city directly across the Rio Grande from El Paso. When he was eight, he moved with his family to Los Angeles, where his love of painting led to his involvement in mural art. Between 1969 and 1973, he pursued a degree in graphic arts at California State University at Los Angeles and studied at Ottis Art Institute in L.A.

The artist has more than twenty years' experience in coordinating, directing, and executing mural art projects in California, Texas, and other areas of the Southwest. Throughout his artistic career, he has held positions as art director, graphic artist, curator, technical consultant, and art instructor. His success as a mural artist and public art advocate have earned him the respect of his peers and a reputation for his expertise in muralism.

Mr. Callejo has played a major role in over thirty-five mural projects, including one in Managua, Nicaragua, in 1986. From 1983 to 1986, he provided training and technical assistance to schools, libraries, and art advocacy groups as a consultant for art projects.

Mr. Callejo's work has been exhibited nationally and internationally and has been published in numerous periodicals, journals, and books. He also has been featured in several television and movie documentaries.

In 1992, he began working on the project of his life: El Paso's largest (5,400 square feet) mural. Carlos was selected to paint a four-wall mural inside the newly constructed county courthouse. He also completed a mural in Tyler, Texas, in 1994 and spent three months in 1995 in Spoleto, Italy courtesy of the Lila Wallace Reader's Digest Arts International Program.

SANDRA CISNEROS
Writer and Poet
(1954–   )

Born in Chicago in 1954, the only daughter among seven children of a Mexican father and a Chicana mother, Sandra Cisneros is a writer with roots firmly in the Hispanic American community. Her family moved frequently between the United States and Mexico because of her father's homesickness for his native land. Despite feeling homeless and displaced, Sandra found comfort in books.

In the late 1970s, Cisneros decided to write about her upbringing, her feelings of alienation, her poverty, and her divided cultural loyalties. *The House on Mango Street* was published in 1983. Esperanza, a character in the book, is a poor Hispanic adolescent who longs for a house she can be proud of and a room of her own. In 1985, this work of fiction was awarded the Before Columbus Foundation American Book Award.

Her third volume of verse, *My Wicked, Wicked Ways*, published in 1987, received critical acclaim.

Published in 1991, her collection of short stories about Mexican-American characters living in the San Antonio, Texas, area, *Woman Hollering Creek and Other Stories*, was chosen as a Noteworthy Book of 1991 by *The New York Times*, and one of the Best Books of 1991 by *The Library Journal*.

In all her works Cisneros addresses important contemporary issues associated with minorities, and incorporates Hispanic dialect and social commentary that reveal feelings unique to Hispanic women. She is also involved in the Human Rights movement, and most recently spearheaded a campaign to pressure the United States and other world powers to intervene in the war in the former Yugoslavia.

JOSE LUIS CUEVAS
Artist
(1934–   )

Cuevas, a Mexican-born painter and illustrator, became obsessed with drawing at an early age. Spending a large part of his childhood confined to a sickbed, he began drawing what he could see from his window. He sketched the street people of Mexico City. Cuevas has said that drawing was "the best vehicle for expressing my daily struggle with death."

At the age of thirteen, Cuevas had his first one-man show. Once known as the "Mexican Boy Wonder," by 1953 he had found his style. Mostly done in ink and watercolors, his drawings reflect the miseries of humanity. He preferred to draw the huddled beggars on the street, the deformed and the grotesque.

Though it has been said that his art is not pretty, Cuevas's paintings and drawings are included in the permanent collection of famous museums around the world, including the Museum of Modern Art in New York and the Philadelphia Museum of Art.

One of the few Mexican artists known outside his own country, he has had one-man shows in Europe, Latin America, and the United States, and has won numerous international drawing awards. Picasso was among those who had Cuevas's work in their private collections.

ROLANDO HINOJOSA-SMITH
Writer
(1929–   )

The dean of Mexican-American writers, Hinojosa-Smith was born on January 21, 1929, in Mercedes, Texas. He is the son of Manuel G. Hinojosa and Carrie E. Smith and grew up in a bilingual household.

He earned his bachelor's degree from the University of Texas at Austin, his master's at New Mexico Highlands University, and his Ph.D. at the University of Illinois. He holds the Ellen Clayton Garwood Professorship and the Mari Sabusawa Michener Chair at the University of Texas at Austin, where he holds the rank of professor in the English department.

Hinojosa-Smith has consulted for the U.S. Information Agency in Panama, Mexico, Iraq, and various European countries. His best-known work, *The Klail City Death Trip Series*, appears in English and Spanish, and parts of it have been translated into Dutch, German, and French. Doctoral and master's theses on his work have been done in this country as well as in Sweden, Italy, France, Germany, and the Netherlands.

In 1973, Hinojosa-Smith was awarded the Premio Quinto Sol for *Estampas del Valle*, and in 1976, the Casa de las Americas Prize for *Klail City y sus alrededores*.

In 1995, he was named outstanding Latino Faculty by the Hispanic Caucus of the American Association of Higher Education.

JOHN QUINONES
ABC News Correspondent
(1952–   )

Quinones was born May 23, 1952, in San Antonio, Texas, son of Bruno and Maria Quinones. He received a B.A. degree in speech communications from St. Mary's University in Texas and received a master's degree from the Columbia School of Journalism.

Mr. Quinones joined ABC News in June 1982 as a general assignment correspondent based in Miami, providing reports for *World News Tonight with Peter Jennings* and other ABC News broadcasts. He was one of the few American journalists reporting from Panama City during the U.S. invasion in December 1989.

Mr. Quinones has reported on a wide range of stories originating from Central America, including the political and economic turmoil in Argentina and civil war in El Salvador. He also covered such stories as the explosion aboard the U.S.S. *Iowa*, the execution of serial killer Ted Bundy, and the debate over the availability of guns in Florida.

Prior to joining ABC News, Mr. Quinones was a reporter with WBBM-TV in Chicago, where he covered such stories as the Haitian boat people in 1982 and the Cuban boat lift in 1980. He won two Emmy Awards for his 1980 reporting on the plight of illegal aliens from Mexico.

In April 1990, Mr. Quinones received a National Emmy Award for his work on the documentary *Burning Questions—The Poisoning of America*. He is the recipient of a Gabriel Award, a World Hunger Media Award, and a Citation from the Robert F. Kennedy Journalism Awards. He received a 1990 Emmy for *Window on the Past*. John was named a correspondent for ABC News *Prime Time Live* in November 1991.

RICHARD RODRIGUEZ
Writer, Teacher
(1944–   )

Born in Sacramento, California, in 1948, Mexican-American Richard Rodriguez attended a Catholic parochial school, where he experienced the difficulties of transition from Spanish to English for a child in an era when bilingual education was not in vogue. He would tap that experience and the lessons it taught him several decades later in a book, *Hunger of Memory: The Education of Richard Rodriguez.*

While he might have had an easier time as a child adjusting to school and English had Spanish also been spoken in the classroom, he argues, it would not have helped him in the long run. In his book he maintains the value of the trauma of adjustment in helping the child cope more effectively with a society in which Spanish is not the primary language. When you begin the educational process, he wrote, you have to leave the family behind and learn your public role. Spanish, of course, would remain his private language, as well as part of his beloved heritage.

Rodriguez did conquer the language barrier and went on to Stanford University, Columbia University, and the University of California at Berkeley, where he earned a Ph.D. in English. He taught for a while at Berkeley but opted for the writer's life as opposed to a full-time professorship.

He writes primarily about Hispanic Americans and the problems they face. The viewpoints he offers are often surprising. Simple answers, he feels, do not often solve complex problems. In 1992, President Bush bestowed on him the Charles Frankel Humanities Award from the National Endowment for the Arts. He now writes for *Harper's*, the *Los Angeles Times Sunday Magazine*, *The New Republic*, and others.

PHIL ROMAN

Animator, Director, Producer
(1930–   )

Born December 21, 1930, in Fresno, California, Roman spoke Spanish until he started kindergarten and learned to express himself in both English and the international language, art. He saw Walt Disney's *Bambi* at a local cinema at age eleven and decided to devote himself to turning drawings into life on the screen.

The farmlands of Fresno produced a gifted Latino artist with a fertile imagination who drew his way from a comic strip in the high school paper to one of the top positions in the colorful but highly competitive field of animation. He received his art training at the Los Angeles Art Center. He found his first job in animation before graduation when he joined the Disney Studios in 1955, starting as an assistant animator on *Sleeping Beauty*.

Three-time Emmy winner Phil Roman has produced and directed animated series, theatricals, and commercials for nearly four decades. Now president and CEO of Film Roman, his is the only independent studio among the major animation producers. His studio currently produces the top-rated series *The Simpsons*, *Bobby's World*, and *Mighty Max*, and has released *Tom and Jerry—The Movie*.

The quality of Film Roman shows can best be demonstrated by the fact that the ten specials he has produced have all garnered Emmy nominations. Three of those ten have won the award.

He has been a finalist in the entertainment category for Los Angeles Entrepreneur of the Year and also in the animation division of the National Cartoonists Society awards competition.

Roman recently finalized a $50 million limited-distribution deal with BetaFilm for European Television. His animation studio will provide all of the 1996 Olympic promos.

His studio (Film Roman) is the only privately held studio producing animated cartoons for Saturday morning, prime-time, first-run syndication, commercials, CD-ROM, and theatrical release.

Despite a low profile, Roman's studio holds its own against such animation giants as Disney.

RUBEN SALAZAR
Journalist
(1928–1970)

Ruben Salazar, born in Ciudad Juárez, Mexico, came to Southern California with his parents as a boy. In 1959, he became a reporter for the *Los Angeles Times*, launching a career that would lead him to martyrdom.

He became the newspaper's correspondent in the Dominican Republic and Vietnam, and later headed its Mexico City bureau. In 1969, he became news director of KMEX, a Spanish-language TV station, but continued to write a weekly column for the *Times* about L.A.'s Mexican community. He applied hard-hitting journalistic techniques to both assignments.

By the summer of 1970, Chicanos in East L.A., upset by the growing number of Hispanics being killed and wounded in Vietnam, were staging their own protest demonstrations, often clashing with police. On August 29, a rally was organized and 100,000 people filled Laguna Park to protest as part of the Chicano National Moratorium on Vietnam. Rocks and bottles were thrown at riot-garbed police, who fired back and made arrests.

Salazar, covering the rally for KMEX, went into a bar with some coworkers. Sheriff's deputies surrounded it and ordered everyone out but fired tear gas projectiles inside. One hit Salazar on the head and killed him.

The death of this Chicano spokesman and the inconclusive investigation that followed created much controversy. Salazar, married with three children, had used blunt language in his reporting, and many thought police were pleased to have silenced him. His articulate voice has been sorely missed in the years that followed.

GARY SOTO
Poet, Author
(1952–   )

Born in Fresno, California, in 1952, Gary Soto has become a literary figure worthy of attention from the major critics of our time. An important poet, he has also written book-length fiction and nonfiction and short film scripts. His writing reflects many facets of his Mexican-American heritage.

Soto earned a Master of Fine Arts degree in creative writing from the University of California at Irvine and teaches at the University of California at Berkeley in the English Department. The honors his work has brought his way include NEA and Guggenheim fellowships plus such literary prizes as the California Library Association's Patricia Beatty Award, the American Book Award of the Before Columbus Foundation, the Bess Hoke Award for Poetry, and the Discovery *The Nation* Prize.

His writing, which taps his own childhood experiences in the San Joaquin Valley, including a migrant worker background, often depicts the poverty and misery common to that life. But, critics note, his characters are not stereotypes of the extremes of despair or heroism, and his themes blend the worldly and the spiritual. His terse, simple style troubles some critics, but there is general recognition that Soto is more than an ethnic poet. His poetry and prose may be rooted in his Hispanic background and experiences, but his images go beyond that to tap something universal that can enlighten all readers.

In 1993, Soto published a children's book, *Local News*, a collection of thirteen stories all set in a Mexican-American neighborhood.

Luis
VALDES
Playwright, Director
(1940–   )

Luis Valdes was born and raised in San Jose, California. The son of migrant farmworkers, Luis had little chance of learning English. However, by the time he had graduated from high school, Valdes had mastered the English language to a point where it even overshadowed his native Spanish.

In the 1960s, Valdes decided to reestablish his ethnic roots, and in doing so he joined the cause of farm labor leader César Chavez and his farmworkers' union. He created a road show called El Teatro Campesino, which traveled with the migrant workers performing Latino-related acts and entertainment.

Eventually, Valdes's efforts and talents were rewarded, as his play *Zoot Suit* was performed on the Broadway stage.

Valdes achieved great success with his movie *La Bamba*, the 1988 film about the life of Mexican rock-and-roll star Ritchie Valens. His work on *La Bamba* established Valdes as a major film director.

In 1992, his Christmas story, *La Pastorela*, was performed on PBS television, starring Linda Ronstadt and Paul Rodriguez. In 1994, Valdez's screen version of the *Cisco Kid*, filmed entirely in Mexico, aired on TNT television.

TOM FLORES

Football Player, General
Manager, Head Coach
(1937–   )

Seahawks

Tom was born in Fresno, California, attended Sanger High
School (its football field is named in his honor), then went on to
Fresno City College and the College of the Pacific, where he let-
tered in football and baseball. As a senior, he ranked fourth in
the nation in total offense.

Tom signed with the Oakland Raiders of the fledging American
Football League as a free agent in 1960. Playing six seasons as
quarterback with the Raiders, he led the AFL in completions
(54.0%) and fewest interceptions in 1960 and finished second to
the Houston Oilers' George Blanda in passing, with 2,176 yards.
Flores passed for six touchdowns against the Houston Oilers on
December 22, 1963, a Raiders record that still stands. In 1967 he
was traded to the Buffalo Bills, where he played two seasons,
earning the starting job only to be felled by a knee injury. In 1969
he joined the Kansas City Chiefs and played two seasons,
including their Super Bowl IV championship team.

Flores is one of only two people in NFL history, along with
former Chicago Bears head coach Mike Ditka, to have a Super
Bowl ring as a player, an assistant coach, and a head coach.

Flores entered into his 36th year in the NFL in 1992. He was
a player for ten seasons with the Oakland Raiders (1960–
61, 1963–66), Buffalo Bills (1967–68), and Kansas City Chiefs
(1969–70). He was an assistant coach with the Buffalo Bills
(1971) and Oakland Raiders (1972–78), head coach of the
Raiders (1979–87), the Seahawks president/general manager
(1989–92), and then as the Seahawks head coach. He retired in
1994.

RUDY
GALINDO
Champion Figure Skater
(1969–   )

Born in San Jose, California, September 9, 1969, Rudy Galindo suffered years of tragedy and hardship in life as well as in his skating career. He lost two coaches to cancer and AIDS, and his father, Jess Galindo, died of a heart attack in 1993. Six months later his brother George died of AIDS.

But on January 20, 1996, at the age of twenty-six, in the performance of his life, Galindo became the first Mexican-American to win the U.S. Figure Skating Championship, and the oldest man to do so since Chris Christenson in 1926. He followed up that success with a third-place finish at the World Championships, a performance that earned him the bronze medal.

His fantastic victory occurred in San Jose in front of a hometown crowd of 11,000, who were all on their feet cheering him on. In the end, Galindo quietly bowed his head to cross himself in honor of his father, brother, and the two coaches he had lost.

Galindo was twice a national pairs champion with Kristi Yamaguchi before she went on to solo success and an Olympic gold medal. Returning to singles skating himself, Galindo placed fifth at the 1993 nationals and fell to seventh in 1994 and eighth in 1995. Galindo says, "I'm always thinking about all the tragedy, but that made me want to see if I could do better."

Galindo owes much of his success to his coach and sister, Laura Galindo, who in 1985 gave up her own dreams of championships to join the Ice Follies and make enough money, she says, to "support my brother's career."

RICHARD ALONZO "PANCHO" GONZALES
Tennis Pro
(1928–1995)

Born in Los Angeles in 1928 to Mexican-born parents, Pancho Gonzalez was an unlikely candidate for stardom in the elite tennis world, then rooted in the country club set. But he parlayed a gift tennis racket, innate skills, lots of practice, and determination into a place at the top of that sport's championship ranks.

Not yet a teen, he was garnering attention as a potential star from the Los Angeles press for his tournament victories. He soon dropped out of school and joined the amateur circuit. While he improved steadily, he didn't hit his stride until after a hitch in the Navy in the mid-1940s. In 1948, he won the U.S. Singles Championship at Forest Hills, New York. By his own admission, that victory turned his head. He stopped training hard and he stopped winning. But stung with poor results, he stopped partying and feuding with the media in time to prepare for that major tournament, and he won it again in 1949.

He turned pro in 1950, in an era when open tennis had not yet been accepted, opting for money over mere fame, with a wife and three kids to feed. He became the professional singles champion of the world, held that title until 1961, and continued to be rated a top ten player into the early 1970s.

He was always quick to show temper but was a fierce competitor with a powerful serve. Long after his active tournament days were over, he could be found working as a teaching pro in Los Angeles.

NANCY LOPEZ
Pro Golfer
(1957–   )

Nancy Lopez was born in Torrance, California, on January 6, 1957, to Domingo and Marina Lopez. Shortly after her birth the family moved to Roswell, New Mexico. When she was eight her father gave her a cut-down four-wood. In less than a year she was playing rounds with him, and by age eleven she was beating him.

Lopez was only twelve when she won the New Mexico Women's Amateur, and in the following years she won the USGA Junior Girls Championship twice (1972 and 1974). She won the Western Junior three times and the Mexican Amateur in 1975. Also in 1975, Lopez entered the U.S. Women's Open as an amateur and finished second. The next year she claimed the AIAW National Championship and was a member of the U.S. Curtis Cup and World Amateur teams.

The 1976 All-American and Tulsa University Female Athlete of the Year turned professional after her sophomore year of college, joining the LPGA in 1977. In 1978 she won nine tournaments, including a record-setting five in a row. That year she was named Rolex Player of the Year and Rookie of the Year and earned the Vare Trophy. The following season she captured eight events and again earned Player of the Year and Vare Trophy honors.

As of 1993, Nancy Lopez had a total of 46 career victories, with career earnings at $3,708,470. She owes much of her success in the game of golf to her father, Domingo, who had coached her seriously from that early age of eight.

PABLO MORALES
Olympic Swimmer
(1964–   )

Born December 5, 1964, in Chicago, Illinois, Pablo Morales has been described as an exceptionally talented athlete driven by an incredible work ethic. He currently holds the world record in the 100-meter butterfly, with a time of 52.84 seconds, a mark which has stood since June of 1986. At the 1984 Summer Olympic Games, Morales won three medals, a gold in the medley relay and silvers in the 100-meter butterfly and the 200-meter individual medley. The winningest swimmer in collegiate history, he captured a record eleven individual NCAA championships, one short of the maximum possible in a four-year career, before graduating in 1987 from Stanford University, whose team he led to three consecutive NCAA titles from 1985–1987.

While at Stanford, Morales gave time and energy to community services for junior high school students and covered women's basketball as a reporter for the college newspaper. He was recognized for these achievements by being named co-winner of the A1 Masters Award, the university's highest honor for athletic performance, leadership, and academic excellence.

In 1988, although the current world record holder, Morales failed by 3/100ths of a second to make the Olympic team. Following a grueling six-month comeback training regimen, Morales not only won the 100-meter butterfly at the 1992 Olympic Trials, but also the support of swimming fans throughout the United States. His incredible rise back to the top of his sport was completed with a moving performance that earned him the individual Olympic gold medal which had eluded him for so long.

ANTHONY MUNOZ
Pro Football Star
(1958–   )

Munoz was born August 19, 1958, in Ontario, California. He was selected All-America offensive tackle at Southern California in 1979, and was a first-round draft pick of the Cincinnati Bengals in 1980.

It has been said that nobody plays tackle better than Anthony Munoz. The Cincinnati Bengals stalwart offensive tackle has been selected to play in the Pro Bowl in 12 of the 16 seasons he's been in the National Football League. The only year he missed was his rookie season in 1980. He is considered by most experts as the best offensive tackle of all time.

Munoz is big, strong, tough, quick, and as talented as anyone who ever has played offensive tackle. He likes to stay in shape by running four miles or so each day from season's end through May.

Munoz won the NFL Man of the Year award for 1991. The award recognizes players who excel as role models both on and off the field. "This is right up at the top of any honor I've ever been given," the All-Pro offensive lineman said. "It means a lot to me because, as a football player, so often you're judged only by what you do on the field. A major part of this award is for things you do as a citizen in your community."

Munoz enjoys children. "My heart really is with youth," he says. "My wife De De and I have two of our own, but I also have gotten involved with youth in the Cincinnati area." He is involved in many charitable community activities, including a drug and alcohol prevention program in schools in the Cincinnati area.

TOMMY NUNEZ
Referee, National Basketball Association

The NBA has a policy of not releasing any information on the referees, but we'll say this. After summer workouts in 1973 at the rookie camps of the Portland Trailblazers and the Milwaukee Bucks, young, hardworking Tommy Nunez became the first Mexican-American to be an official in any major-league sport in the United States.

Wish we were free to say more!

ATHLETES

JIM PLUNKETT
Pro Quarterback
(1947–   )

Born in San Jose, California, in 1947 to poor parents of Mexican ancestry who spoke only English to their children, James William Plunkett, Jr., grew up unfamiliar with Spanish. By the age of ten, he was interested in sports and was a Stanford University football fan. Despite a bone and ligament ailment, he was drawn to football and became a star high school quarterback, as well as the student body president.

Though heavily recruited by colleges, he chose nearby Stanford. Weakened from a neck operation, he did not play well as a freshman and was "redshirted" as the number-three quarterback the next year. When he did finally make the varsity in 1968, he began racking up the yardage that was to make him famous, though he played injured part of the time. In 1970, he led his team to a Rose Bowl upset victory and won both the Heisman and Maxwell trophies.

He was drafted by the New England Patriots pro team and won Rookie of the Year honors. Playing with a weak team led to physical problems for Jim Plunkett. He was traded to the San Francisco Forty-Niners, where his problems continued, and he was released a year later. The Oakland Raiders picked him up, and by 1980 he was able to move into the top quarterback spot and to lead the team to a Super Bowl victory. He became symbolic of the canny veteran who figures out, somehow, how to win. His belief in hard work and not giving up paid off. He won Comeback Player of the Year pro honors in 1980. Following his retirement in 1992, he entered the broadcast booth, where he works as an Oakland Raiders radio announcer.

LEE TREVINO
Golf Pro
(1939–)

Seeing Lee Trevino grow up in a four-room shack near Dallas, Texas, one would never have guessed that he would become a master at a rich man's game. Raised by his mother and grandfather, Trevino spent a lot of his playtime at a nearby golf course hunting golf balls to make extra money. One day he found the head of an old five-iron, which he fitted with a homemade shaft. By the age of six, he was playing on a two-hole golf course he had made himself.

Trevino quit school after the eighth grade to help support his family. He worked at various golf courses and driving ranges near his home. At seventeen, he joined the Marines. He spent a tour in the Far East. During a two-year reenlistment, he became the golf champion of the Marine Corps.

In 1965, Trevino won the Texas State Open and a year later joined the PGA. Since 1968, "Supermex," as he calls himself, has finished in the top ten in fifty PGA tournaments. He played for the U.S. team on two Ryder Cup and three World Cup teams. During one month in 1971, Trevino won three national championships. *Sports Illustrated* named him Sportsman of the Year. In 1971, he became the first golfer in history to win the British, Canadian, and U.S. Open in the same year.

Trevino enjoys charity work. He donates time and money and has said, "I don't believe in helping just one race or nationality, I'm only concerned with the poor—black, white, yellow, red— and the young."

FERNANDO VALENZUELA
Baseball Player
(1960–   )

The seventh son and youngest of twelve children, Fernando Valenzuela was born in the state of Sonora, Mexico, on November 1, 1960. The family home was a four-room adobe dwelling in the village of Etchohuaquila. Valenzuela began playing baseball on the village team with his brothers. Some time between the ages of twelve and sixteen, he left school to concentrate on baseball full-time. While playing in the Mexican League, he attracted the attention of major-league scouts and was signed by the Los Angeles Dodgers in 1979.

To supplement Valenzuela's fastball and curveball, the Dodgers had Mexican-American relief pitcher Bob Costello teach him to throw the screwball, the pitch that brought him to the top of the baseball world.

On April 8, 1981, Valenzuela became the first rookie ever to start for Los Angeles on opening day, dazzling the fans by pitching a five-hit shutout against the defending National League West champion Astros. His efforts that season helped the Dodgers win the World Series.

In November 1981, Valenzuela became the first rookie to win the Cy Young Award. In December 1981 he was named the National League Rookie of the Year, becoming the first player ever to win that honor and the Cy Young in the same year.

Valenzuela played with the Dodgers through ten seasons. He was signed by the American League Baltimore Orioles for the 1993 season. He now pitches for the San Diego Padres.

JESSE AGUIRRE
Corporate Executive
(1944–   )

Mr. Aguirre was born June 3, 1944, in Coleman, Texas, and now resides in St. Louis, Missouri. He received his B.A. at Stanford University in June 1970, and his M.A. at Harvard Law School in June 1975.

Aguirre interned with the Colorado public defender's office and was associated with law firms in California. From 1975 until 1977, he helped direct the Latin American Teaching Fellowship Program in São Paulo, Brazil, and Bogotá, Colombia.

Aguirre is vice president of corporate relations for Anheuser-Busch, parent company of the world's largest brewer. He was named to this position in 1984. Aguirre is responsible for coordination of programs and activities with national and state public interest organizations concerning a variety of issues, including community development and certain legislative activities in conjunction with the company's Industry and Government Affairs Department.

Aguirre is a member of the Anheuser-Busch board of directors. He is also vice president of the board of directors of the National Hispanic Scholarship Fund, and a member of the board of directors of the Arts and Education Council of St. Louis.

He is responsible for his company's programs with the Hispanic community, provides advice and counsel to all parts of the company on Hispanic issues, designs and implements programs for Hispanic contracts and the company's nationwide Hispanic outreach program.

GRACE FLORES-HUGHES

Businesswoman
(1946–   )

Grace Flores-Hughes was born in Taft, Texas, on June 11, 1946. She received her B.A. degree from the University of the District of Columbia and her M.A. from Harvard University.

Ms. Flores-Hughes began a twenty-year career with the federal workforce as a GS-2 at the Kelly Air Force Base in Texas. Over the years she has held numerous positions including associate administrator at the Small Business Administration, and director, community relations service, at the Department of Justice. She has also been a visiting professor in the Department of Political Science at the University of Nebraska at Omaha and at Nebraska Wesleyan University.

Ms. Flores-Hughes is currently the president of Grace, Inc., of Virginia. In this capacity, she has lectured to a variety of audiences nationwide on topics that address ways in which the private and public sectors can achieve a diverse workforce and peaceful and just settlements of disputes related to racial and ethnic conflict. She has also written numerous articles on these subjects which have appeared in leading business magazines.

Ms. Flores-Hughes has been named one of the hundred most influential Hispanics in the United States by *Hispanic Business Magazine*. She has received numerous awards, including the 1990 Outstanding Public Service Award presented by the national capital area chapter of the American Society for Public Administration. She currently chairs the executive advisory board of the *Journal of Hispanic Policy* at the Kennedy School of Government at Harvard University.

ESTEVAN OCHOA
Businessman, Municipal Leader
(1831–1888)

Estevan Ochoa was born in Chihuahua, Mexico, in 1831 and was reared with an understanding of his father's shipping business, which spanned northern Mexico and America's Southwest. It came as no surprise that he would carve out his own career in that field during the mid-nineteenth-century boom in the inland freight delivery business, using pack mules and wagon trains to transport goods inland.

He settled in Tucson, Arizona, and by the end of the Civil War headed a major shipping enterprise with partner P. R. Tully, a business that included a retail operation which supplied both the city and the more remote areas in the region with supplies. The firm eventually expanded into mining and sheep ranching. Ochoa was an acknowledged leader in the community, admired by both Anglos and Hispanics, and he and his wife entertained lavishly.

Unlike many towns in the Southwest, Tucson was hospitable to native Hispanics and newcomers from Mexico. Indeed, these people played a major role in the community's business, political, cultural, and educational life. Ochoa, who was elected mayor in 1875, led the fight for Arizona's public school system; he believed Mexicans who wanted to prosper in the United States needed to learn English. He and his fellow Hispanics, mostly Catholic, also started private and parochial schools.

When railroads took over, Ochoa was caught short and his business suffered, but not his personal reputation.

REYNALDO (REYNIE) U. ORTIZ

Corporate Executive
(1946–   )

Mr. Ortiz was born on October 24, 1946, in New Mexico. Married with three children, he now lives in Denver, Colorado.

Mr. Ortiz's educational background includes a Stanford University Sloan Fellowship, an appointment by the CEO of IBM Corporation, in which he obtained a master of science in management in 1984. In May 1991, Mr. Ortiz was honored with a doctorate of law *honoris causa* from New Mexico State for his outstanding professional achievements. In the same year, he also received the Hispanic Engineering National Professional Achievement in Industry Award.

Mr. Ortiz accepted an appointment by the U.S. Secretary of Commerce to serve on the department's Minority Enterprise Development Advisory Council and is a member of the National Advisory Council of the Small Business Administration. He also serves on the President's Council on Rural America, a position President George Bush appointed him to in March 1991.

Before joining U.S. West Ventures Group in 1986, Mr. Ortiz was employed for sixteen years by IBM, where he established an outstanding leadership record in the management of worldwide manufacturing, engineering, and marketing business organizations. Prior to his current corporate appointment as vice president, corporate public policy, at U.S. West, he was president and CEO of U.S. West New Vector Group, a subsidiary providing wireless communications services in over forty-eight U.S. markets in a fifteen-state region and over sixty paging systems in a thirteen-state region.

Presently, he works as an executive with Jones Intercable of Colorado.

FRANCISCO RAMIREZ
Editor, Publisher
(1830–1890)

Francisco Ramirez was born in 1830 to a family destined to lose land, cattle, dignity, and control of their lives when westward-expanding Americans took over California. That occurred in the 1840s, and within a decade the young Ramirez would provide a journalistic voice for his Spanish-speaking compatriots.

He launched his newspaper career as a typesetter for the *Los Angeles Star*'s Spanish page. Upset by that paper's editorials, which he felt were unfair, he quit in 1855 to start L.A.'s first Spanish-language newspaper, *El Clamor Público*, which became widely read.

Ramirez went beyond politics to cover the history of the California region, the state's potential, even the slavery question back east that was pushing the nation toward war. He insisted that "American" applied to everyone in the Western Hemisphere, not just to the Anglos. While stressing Hispanic pride by reminding his readers what they had accomplished in the land, he encouraged them to teach their children English as well as Spanish, or to move to Mexico or Latin America.

He ran for city assembly in 1859 but won only 25 percent of the vote. He was crushed, and not much later, his newspaper failed. His attacks on U.S. policies had alienated Anglo advertisers and his hard line was out of step with most of his readers. Ramirez went to Mexico to live and held several government positions there. This pioneer in his field had one more brief fling with a newspaper before disappearing from public view.

EVERETT ALVAREZ, JR.
Navy Pilot, Leader
(1937–   )

Of Mexican extraction, Everett Alvarez, Jr., was born in Salinas, California, in 1937. The first in his family to get a college education, he decided after graduation from the University of Santa Clara to join the navy and become a pilot.

The Vietnam War tested his courage. When the North Vietnamese attacked two navy ships in 1964, Alvarez was one of the pilots sent to retaliate. His plane was hit and he parachuted into the Gulf of Tonkin waters, where he was captured, becoming the first U.S. prisoner of war in that conflict. For nearly nine years, he coped with the horrors of North Vietnamese prison camps, tapping the same survival instincts his migrant worker grandparents had needed to persevere here decades earlier.

After a peace agreement was reached between Hanoi and Washington, he was released and returned home to parades and honors befitting a hero. He had earned a Distinguished Flying Cross, two Purple Hearts, two Legions of Merit, and an invitation to the White House. Alvarez continued his military career, earned a law degree at George Washington University, and married. He has two children.

When he ended his Navy career, he was appointed deputy director of the Peace Corps and subsequently was named deputy administrator of the Veterans Administration. When the Vietnam Veterans Memorial was dedicated in Washington in 1982, Alvarez was asked to speak. As a survivor, he praised the courage of those who perished.

Luis
ALVAREZ
Master Scientist
(1911–1988)

Associates of Luis Alvarez were not surprised when he was awarded the Nobel Prize in 1968. One colleague wrote of Luis "he was the most imaginative, creative, and inventive scientist I ever encountered. . . . He loved more than anything doing something that everyone else found impossible."

Alvarez received his doctoral degree in physics in 1936 and began teaching at the University of California at Berkeley. He worked at the Radiation Laboratory at MIT from 1940 to 1943, where he helped develop microwave beacons, linear radar antennas, and a ground-controlled landing approach system to facilitate aircraft landings under adverse weather conditions.

During 1944–45, Alvarez worked at Los Alamos, New Mexico, on the development of the atomic bomb. On August 6, 1945, he flew as a scientific observer in the B-29 which followed the *Enola Gay* when it dropped the bomb on Hiroshima.

After the war, Dr. Alvarez returned to teaching and research at Berkeley. In 1968 he was awarded the Nobel Prize in physics for his research using bubble chambers to detect new subatomic particles.

In 1980, Dr. Alvarez and his son, geologist Walter Alvarez, wrote a controversial article theorizing that the extinction of the dinosaurs was caused by a giant meteorite's striking the earth.

The science world mourned the loss of Dr. Alvarez upon his death in 1988.

RAUL HECTOR CASTRO
Politician, Leader
(1916–1977)

Raul Hector Castro was born in Cananea, Mexico, just fifty miles south of the Arizona border. He shared a one-room house with his parents and twelve other children.

His father, wanting a better life for his family, moved to Arizona. With the move came much prejudice and continued poverty.

In the 1930s, young Castro toiled at being a boxer, farmhand, and copper miner to pay for his education at Northern Arizona University, graduating in 1939. After working for the State Department for six years, Castro decided he needed a broader background in law. He returned to school and received his law degree in 1949.

Mr. Castro was a prosecuting attorney from 1949 to 1964, also serving as a county attorney and superior court judge. Other prestigious assignments included American ambassador to El Salvador (1964–1968), and American ambassador to Bolivia (1968–1969).

Commenting on his long climb from an early life of poverty and prejudice, Castro stated "Ever since I was little, I've been told, 'Raul, you haven't got a chance . . .' Well, I've been lots of places for a guy who didn't have a chance. I can't perform miracles, but adversity is my angel."

Castro served as governor of Arizona from 1975 to 1977.

CESAR CHAVEZ
Farm Labor Leader
(1927–1993)

Cesar Chavez spent most of his life fighting to improve the working conditions of migrant farmworkers. Chavez's family had gone to California during the Great Depression, having heard that they could earn a good living working at large farms in the state. They ended up in a one-room shack with no running water or electricity. Even the children were expected to work from morning to night. The family moved so often that by the time Chavez finished the eighth grade, he had been enrolled in thirty-six different schools.

Chavez left school after the eighth grade and began working in the vineyards of California. He enlisted in the Navy during World War II.

After the war, Chavez returned to the farms and began his fight on behalf of the Hispanic farmworkers. In 1962, he founded the National Farm Workers Association. He traveled throughout California convincing laborers to join. By 1965, the union had grown substantially, and with their demand for pay raises being squelched by the growers came the strikes and the call for boycotts across America. Chavez received encouragement from Martin Luther King, Jr., Robert F. Kennedy, and Pope Paul VI, among others.

In 1970, after five years of struggle, the grape growers finally agreed to the union contract. The union became the United Farm Workers and joined the AFL-CIO.

Cesar Chavez passed away at his home near Yuma, Arizona, April 23, 1993.

PATRICK FERNANDEZ FLORES
Archbishop
(1929–)

Patrick Flores is the archbishop of the San Antonio, Texas, diocese. He is the first Mexican-American to reach such a high position in the Roman Catholic church. He was born July 26, 1929, in Ganado, Texas, the seventh of nine children.

After finishing Kirwin High School, Galveston, he entered St. Mary's Seminary (1949) in La Porte, Texas, and later attended St. Mary's Seminary in Houston. On May 26, 1956, he was ordained to the Catholic priesthood by Bishop Wendelin Nold in St. Mary's Cathedral, Galveston.

On March 18, 1970, Pope Paul VI appointed him to serve as auxiliary to the archbishop of San Antonio. In 1972 Bishop Flores was instrumental in establishing the Mexican American Cultural Center in San Antonio, of which he serves as honorary chairman. He also founded the National Foundation for Mexican-American Vocations and the National Hispanic Scholarship Fund.

Patrick Flores has used his influence as bishop to work for many worthwhile causes. He has devoted most of his attention to Mexican-Americans, farmworkers, and the young. In 1976 he cofounded Telethon Navideno to help the needy of San Antonio and surrounding areas in extreme emergencies.

In 1986, Bishop Patrick Flores was awarded the Medal of Freedom.

HECTOR P. GARCIA

Founder American G.I. Forum
(1914–   )

Dr. Hector Garcia was born in Mexico on January 17, 1914. In 1936, he graduated from the University of Texas, and in 1940, received his Doctor of Medicine. His internship was at St. Joseph's Hospital in Omaha, Nebraska.

During World War II, Dr. Garcia served in Europe as a distinguished combat surgeon, being awarded the Bronze Star with six Battle Stars. Upon returning home after the war, he noticed the insults endured by Mexican-American veterans and their lack of government benefits. The last straw came when in 1948 a Texas undertaker refused to bury the remains of Felix Longoria, a Mexican-American soldier killed in the Battle of the Philippines. President Truman, upset by this incident, arranged for Sgt. Longoria to be buried at Arlington National Cemetery.

This case caused Dr. Garcia to vow such treatment of Mexican-Americans wouldn't happen again—not if he could help it. In 1948, he organized the American G.I. Forum, whose mission was specifically to help Mexican-American veterans get the same services as other vets.

Dr. Garcia, who was chairman of the board of the forum, organized more than a hundred chapters in Texas alone. Soon there were G.I. Forum members all over the United States. By the 1950s, the group employed a full-time lobbyist in Washington, D.C.

The G.I. Forum has moved beyond its original purpose of supporting veterans and now speaks out on civil rights issues, hoping to encourage more understanding among all ethnic and religious groups.

Dr. Garcia has served on a number of diplomatic posts, including alternate delegate to the UN. He has worked as a consultant to presidents Kennedy, Johnson, and Carter. Among his numerous awards is the Presidential Medal of Freedom, America's highest civilian honor.

HENRY B. GONZALEZ

United States Representative
(1916–)

Henry Barbosa Gonzalez was born on May 3, 1916, in San Antonio, Texas. His parents had fled Mexico during the 1911 revolution and settled in Texas, where his father became managing editor of *La Prensa*. Gonzalez began working while still in grade school and, like most Mexican-Americans of that era, suffered the indignities of racial prejudice. Having had his college education interrupted during the Depression due to lack of funds, Gonzalez finally graduated from St. Mary's University School of Law in 1943.

Instead of practicing law, Gonzalez held several jobs before becoming active in politics. In 1958, Gonzalez became the first Mexican-American in more than a century to be elected to the Texas state senate. During his years in the Texas legislature, Gonzalez fought against racial segregation and once filibustered for thirty-six hours against a set of bills designed to perpetuate that segregation. In 1961, Gonzalez was elected to the U.S. House of Representatives, the first Mexican-American from Texas ever elected to national office. Gonzalez has been a champion for minority causes since his early days in the House. He has sponsored bills supporting adult basic education, abolition of the poll tax, civil service salary increases, Puerto Rican rights, and the minimum wage, and worked hard to defeat the "bracero" bill in 1964.

Henry Gonzalez has served on many important House committees in his more than thirty years of service, including the chairmanship of the Banking, Finance, and Urban Affairs Committee. He also oversaw the drafting of the savings and loan bailout bill signed by President Bush in 1989.

FATHER ANTONIO JOSÉ MARTÍNEZ

Priest, Educator

(1793–1867)

Born in Abiquiu, territory of New Mexico, in 1793, Antonio José Martínez grew up to be a Catholic priest, a scholar, an educator, and the sort of tough character only a rapidly changing frontier area could spawn.

He arrived in Taos in 1820 and established himself as a popular leader of his parish, a man dedicated to the welfare of the people. A little more than a decade later, after the territory passed from Spanish to Mexican control, money for public schools from a voluntary sin tax on dance halls and bars was nonexistent. So Padre Martínez started a school in which he was the sole teacher. He bought a printing press and produced textbooks, Bibles, and pamphlets. According to rumor, he even became involved in political matters, not excluding such violent incidents as the Taos Uprising in 1847, during which the U.S. territorial governor was killed. The padre, a man of legendary forcefulness, exercised near-dictatorial power in his parish.

He was challenged by Archbishop Jean-Baptiste Lamy, a French churchman sent to New Mexico in 1851 to bring order and discipline to the churches there. The clash between priest and archbishop was chronicled by Willa Cather in her novel *Death Comes for the Archbishop*.

Lamy had the priest excommunicated, but Padre Martínez formed his own church and continued to function as a priest.

GLORIA MOLINA
Politician
(1948–   )

Gloria Molina, the outspoken daughter of a Mexican immigrant laborer, has been named by *Working Women* magazine as "one of the ten women of power to watch in the nineties." *Time* magazine referred to her as "one of the nation's most prominent Hispanic politicians." Molina has been active in California politics since 1982, when she was elected state assemblywoman for the 56th Los Angeles (L.A.) district. In 1987, she was elected to the L.A. city council from the first district. Molina served in this capacity until 1991, when she was elected to the L.A. county board of supervisors. Molina is the first Latina in history to be elected to the California state legislature, the L.A. city council, and the L.A. county board of supervisors.

As county supervisor, Molina controls a new district established by a federal court in 1990 to give Hispanics in L.A. more voting power.

Before running for public office, Molina was deputy for presidential personnel in the Carter administration White House, and served as deputy director for the Department of Health and Human Services in San Francisco.

Molina is known for her candor, independence, issue-oriented style, and stand on the side of the average citizen against almost insurmountable odds. She has developed a reputation as a watchdog for taxpayers' dollars and fiscal responsibility.

In addition to her duties on the board of supervisors, Molina serves on the boards of several organizations including the National Association of Latino Elected Officials, the Mexican American Legal Defense and Educational Project, and the National Hispanic Leadership Agenda.

ELLEN OCHOA

Astronaut

(1959–   )

Born in La Mesa, California, in 1959, Ellen Ochoa graduated from San Diego State University and went on to earn a master's and doctoral degree in electrical engineering from Stanford University.

In 1990, surviving a selection process that began with two thousand applicants, she became the first Hispanic woman chosen by NASA to become an astronaut. Three years later, she orbited the earth in the *Discovery* shuttle, supervising research into the chemical composition of the upper atmosphere, ozone layer depletion, and changes in the sun's radiation level.

Even before this, she had made her mark, first as a researcher at Sandia National Laboratories in Livermore, California, developing and patenting optical techniques for use in space and industry, and then at NASA's Ames Research Center, Moffett Field, California, where she rose to chief of the intelligent systems technology branch.

Dr. Ochoa did not find her Mexican heritage as much of a hurdle as her gender in her technical educational pursuits, with advisers tending to steer her away from "hard" math and engineering. She is married to a computer engineer and is adept at playing the flute. She enjoys lecturing to students, especially Hispanics, about the need to study and work hard to achieve life's goals. She received the 1989 Hispanic Engineer National Achievement Award as Most Promising Engineer in Government and the 1990 National Hispanic Quincentennial Commission Pride Award a year later.

FEDERICO F. PEÑA

U.S. Secretary of Transportation
(1947–   )

Federico Peña was born in 1947 in Laredo, Texas, the third of six children of a cotton broker. He graduated from the University of Texas at Austin in 1968 and earned his law degree there in 1972. He is married to attorney and world-class marathoner Ellen Hart. They have two children.

Prior to becoming the first Hispanic elected to lead Colorado's largest city, he served in that state's legislature for four years. In his second term, Pena, through his political and administrative skills, was elevated to minority leader by his peers. He became much involved with transportation and planning decisions statewide.

As mayor of Denver, one of his greatest accomplishments was gaining approval for construction of one of the largest airports in the world.

Mr. Peña was nominated by President-elect Clinton on December 24, 1992, to head the United States Department of Transportation. He was confirmed by the Senate and sworn in as the twelfth Secretary of Transportation on January 21, 1993.

His future-oriented approach to the national transportation system can fundamentally improve our quality of life, national economy, and global competitiveness.

EDWARD R. ROYBAL

**U.S. Congressman
(1916–   )**

Edward R. Roybal was only four when his family moved from Albuquerque, New Mexico, to a barrio on the east side of Los Angeles in 1920. He entered Roosevelt High School about the time the country was hit hard by the Great Depression. Like a lot of families, the Roybals did not have much money. But Roybal had something on his side—a fierce determination to succeed.

Working hard at odd jobs, he attended the University of California in Los Angeles. His career began in 1940 as a health educator for the California Tuberculosis Association and he subsequently became the director of health education for the Los Angeles County Tuberculosis and Health Association.

Edward R. Roybal took the oath of office to serve in the 88th Congress on January 9, 1963. Prior to his election to the House of Representatives, he served in the Los Angeles city council from 1949 through 1962.

Mr. Roybal serves on several prestigious congressional committees, including the Appropriations Committee, Postal Service and Treasury. He is one of the ranking members on the Labor, Health and Human Services, Education Subcommittee.

A member of the Select Committee on Aging since its inception, Congressman Roybal assumed its chairmanship in 1983. He is widely recognized as a national leader in securing adequate health care and housing for older Americans.

After three decades as a representative, he stunned his constituents by choosing not to run for reelection in 1992.

LUCILLE ROYBAL-ALLARD
U.S. Congresswoman
(1941–   )

Born and raised in Boyle Heights, California, the congresswoman is the eldest daughter of retired Congressman Edward R. Roybal, who served as a member of Congress for thirty years.

Congresswoman Roybal-Allard was elected to represent California's 33rd Congressional District in November 1992. The heavily Latino district includes the cities of Bell, Bell Gardens, Commerce, Cudahy, Huntington Park, Maywood, South Gate, Vernon, the unincorporated areas of Walnut Park and Florence-Firestone, a portion of East Los Angeles and within the city of Los Angeles, Boyle Heights, the metropolitan downtown, Little Tokyo, Chinatown, Pico Union, Filipino Town, and a portion of Koreatown and Westlake.

She is the first Mexican-American woman elected to the U.S. House of Representatives. She has been appointed to serve on the House Committee on Banking, Finance, and Urban Affairs, and the Small Business Committee. Recognizing her leadership abilities, her fellow members of Congress elected her vice president of the freshman congressional class and vice president of the Congressional Hispanic Caucus.

Prior to her election to Congress, she represented the 56th District in the California State Assembly for three terms, serving on a number of important fiscal and policy committees. During her tenure in the assembly, Roybal-Allard distinguished herself as a leader in the legislature and in her community. Through her effort, construction of a toxic waste incinerator in Vernon was halted. She also won passage of the first statute in the nation that established licensure discipline for sexual misconduct by attorneys.

MARIANO GUADALUPE VALLEJO
General, Rancher
(1808–1890)

Born in Monterey, California, in 1808, Mariano Guadalupe Vallejo joined the Mexican army at age sixteen and earned rapid advancement. Liberal for his time, he approved the breakup of the powerful Franciscan missions, which controlled most of California. When their lands and livestock were finally given away, Vallejo took his share. His cattle ranches in Petaluma and Sonoma made him one of California's wealthiest landowners.

In 1833, Vallejo supported a friend, José Figueroa, who wanted to be Mexico's next governor of California. In turn, the new governor named Vallejo commander general of California's northern region. Vallejo set up a garrison in Sonoma and organized the frontier against Indian attacks. When Figueroa died two years later, Vallejo supported his nephew, Juan Batista Alvarado, for governor against a man chosen by the Mexicans. It led to a brief skirmish that resulted in California being named a free state by Mexico.

Soon Alvarado was feuding with his uncle about his encouragement of American settlers in Northern California. Vallejo felt the tide could not be stemmed anyway.

In 1846, the Americans staged the Black Bear Revolt, capturing and imprisoning Vallejo and Alvarado in Fort Sutter. American troops soon took over all of California.

An embittered Vallejo did serve in the state senate for one term but spent his final years concentrating on his family and the wine industry he helped form in Sonoma and the Napa Valley.

TIBIRICO VASQUEZ
Revolutionary
(1845–1875)

Born in 1845 in the southern part of California, Tibirico Vasquez grew up in an era of resentment among native Mexican Californios at having lost control of what once had been theirs. He became what today would be called a guerrilla freedom fighter, the Hollywood stereotype of a bandido who would ambush stagecoaches headed for Los Angeles or San Diego and rob Anglo-American passengers of their valuables.

He viewed it as just retribution, using the wealth of those who had taken California away from its true owners to finance himself and his men. While some Mexicans had moved to Mexico and others tried to live in harmony with the new order, Vasquez fought back with hit-and-run warfare. As a descendant of the earliest Mexican settlers of El Pueblo de la Reina de los Angeles, who had become landowners but had lost their ranches in the transition to Anglo control, he must have felt a bitter sense of loss of the life that might have been.

To California authorities, he was an outright criminal. State Sheriff Billy Rowland vowed to stop him and the federal government offered an $8,000 reward for the capture of Vasquez. The money tempted one of his men, who betrayed Vasquez's mountain hideaway. When he tried to escape, Vasquez was wounded by Rowland's men.

In Los Angeles's city jail, he was treated as a hero by noted visitors. A jury found him guilty of robbery and murder, and he was hanged in 1875, the last of the Mexican bandidos.

JOAN BAEZ
American Folksinger
(1941–   )

Joan Baez was born in New York City on January 9, 1941. Her father was a Mexican-born physicist and educator, and when he was teaching at Harvard, folksinger friends in Boston taught Baez to play the guitar and various styles of folk songs, blues, ballads, and spirituals. She began singing in Boston coffeehouses in the late 1950s.

Her lovely soprano voice caught the attention of a music promoter. Soon she was invited to appear at the Newport, Rhode Island, folk festival, where she made a tremendous impression on the audience. She appeared there again in 1960 and received several offers from record companies to produce her first album. By the mid-1960s, she had become well known not only for her traditional folk ballads, but also for her contemporary protest songs. She stirred America's younger generation with her renditions of "Blowing in the Wind" and "We Shall Overcome."

In 1974, Baez dedicated her Spanish-language album *Gracias a la Vida* to her father, Alberto Baez. In her dedication, Baez wrote that her father "gave me my Latin name and whatever optimism about life I may claim to have."

In 1993, she revived her career with the album *Play Me Backwards*, her first major label release in years. She continues to work tirelessly for social causes.

Baez's career has spanned the decades. She can truly be called the Queen of Folk Music.

VIKKI CARR

Singer
(1942–   )

Born Florencia Bisenta de Casillas Martinez Cardona in El Paso, Texas, Carr began singing in her elementary school shows. After high school, her first singing job was as soloist "Carlita" with the Pepe Callahan Mexican-Irish Band. Wanting to sound more all-American, she changed her name by taking her saint's name, Bisenta (Vikki in English), and shortening her father's name, Cardona, to Carr.

She later signed a recording contract with Liberty Records. Despite the fact that American audiences seemed slow to accept her, she enjoyed great success while touring Australia and, later, England. In 1967 Carr was invited to sing for Queen Elizabeth at a Royal Command Performance. She was the first female Mexican-American singer to be so honored. In 1970 she was voted Woman of the Year by the *Los Angeles Times* for her efforts on behalf of young Mexican-Americans.

Carr has appeared on numerous national television shows, including Johnny Carson and Carol Burnett. She has also been invited to sing at the White House. In 1972, Carr was named Singer of the Year by the American Guild of Variety Artists. Her 1992 album, *Cosas del Amor*, won her a Grammy Award for best Latin pop performance. Carr has recorded over fifty albums, seventeen of which went gold. In 1971, she established the Vikki Carr Scholarship Fund. Over the years this fund has provided the means for many worthy Mexican-American young people to obtain an education.

LYNDA CARTER

Actress, Businesswoman
(1951–   )

Carter was born in Phoenix, Arizona, July 24, 1951. Encouraged by her mother at an early age to explore her natural talents, Carter began singing in high school musicals, then traveled for three years with a nightclub band before realizing the limits in that field.

In the 1970s, she won the Miss World USA crown. Her very first acting break would launch her toward international recognition, cast as the star of a new television series, *Wonder Woman*. In 1984, Carter would star with Loni Anderson in another well-received series, NBC's *Partners in Crime*.

As her career gained momentum, Carter earned roles in substantial television projects. These included *Born to be Sold*, CBS movie-of-the-week *Mickey Spillane's Mike Hammer*, and the coveted title role of CBS's *Rita Hayworth: The Love Goddess*.

Through the 1980s, Carter also delighted television audiences with her singing and dancing talents in numerous specials, earning an Emmy for *Lynda Carter Celebration*.

Now living in Washington, D.C., and having dedicated four years to the demands of motherhood, Carter returned to television in 1992.

Her own company, Lynda Carter Productions, produces compelling projects with strong female leads, is currently developing a number of new projects. The highly rated suspense thriller *Stillwatch* for CBS was one of her successful dramas.

She costarred in the 1994–1995 series *Hawkeye*. In 1996, she starred in two made-for-television movies, *Secret Between Friends* (NBC) and *She Woke Up Pregnant* (ABC), costarring Joe Penny and Theresa Saldana. Her awards include "Hispanic Woman of the Year," from the Hispanic Women's Council; "Most Beautiful Woman of the Year," from the International Academy of Beauty; and Mexico's Aeriel Award as "International Entertainer of the Year," as well as many awards in volunteerism.

EVELYN CISNEROS
Prima Ballerina
(1958–   )

Born in Huntington Beach, California, in 1958, Evelyn Cisneros learned at an early age the burden of being "different." As the only Mexican-American in her school, she was a target for teasing and stares. When Cisneros became shy and fearful, her mother suggested she take ballet lessons.

The demanding classes proved to be not only fun and a boost to her self-confidence but a career stepping-stone as well. Her dance teacher, impressed by her looks and grace, pushed her. Weekly lessons became daily lessons, with Cisneros teaching some beginning classes to cover the costs. In addition, she performed at night.

By fourteen, she made a full commitment to ballet, which meant turning her back on normal teenage pursuits. After school, she would take lessons and practice. In the evenings, she went to Los Angeles, where she danced at the Pacific Ballet Theater. She won a summer scholarship at the San Francisco Ballet School, eventually becoming an apprentice there. In 1976, she moved to San Francisco and within a year became a regular member of that company, though still nineteen.

Impressed by her technique and beauty, the company's artistic director created a ballet for her about the mistreatment of American Indians. In the eighties, she danced *The Tempest* on national television and performed at the White House for President and Mrs. Reagan. When she talks to Hispanic children about her own career, she stresses the rewards of determination and hard work.

Cisneros is a regular member of the dance company of the San Francisco Ballet.

RICARDO MONTALBAN

Actor
(1920–   )

Ricardo Montalban was born November 25, 1920, in Mexico City, Mexico, son of Ricarda and Jenaro. He married Georgiana Young in 1944 and has four children.

His movie career spans almost fifty years, with films including *Fiesta*, in 1947; *Neptune's Daughter*, 1949; *Battleground*, 1950; *Latin Lovers*, 1954; *Sayonara*, 1957; *Cheyenne Autumn*, 1964; *Madame X*, 1966; *Sweet Charity*, 1968; *Escape from the Planet of the Apes*, 1972; *Joe Panther*, 1976; *Star Trek II: The Wrath of Khan*, 1982; and *Cannonball II*, 1986.

He starred in the successful television series *Fantasy Island* and, later, on *Dynasty*. He also played in numerous television features and series appearances. In television commercials, he was spokesperson for the Chrysler Corporation.

The Nosotros founder received an Emmy Award in 1979 for his role in *How the West Was Won*. Montalban won the Golden Aztec Award in 1988. In 1992, he won the Latino Entertainers Lifetime Achievement Award.

RAMON NOVARRO
Pioneer Movie Star
(1899–1968)

Born Ramon Samaniegos in Durango, Mexico, on February 6, 1899, Novarro fled with his family to America during the 1916 Huerta revolution. As a young man, he ventured east to New York to seek his fortune, but only reached the heights of being a busboy in a Times Square automat. Disappointed, Novarro returned to Hollywood and got a job as an usher at a movie house, enjoying films so much that he decided to be an actor.

Novarro spent four years as an obscure dress extra until someone noticed he looked a lot like the megastar Rudolph Valentino. His big break came when Rex Ingram cast him as Rupert of Hentzau in Metro's *Prisoner of Zenda* in 1922.

With the popularity hype of Valentino rubbing off on Novarro, he became known as "Ravishing Ramon," and the Hollywood tourists were buying "secret maps" of the rising star's hideaway.

In 1926 he replaced George Walsh in the title role of *Ben-Hur*, the most ambitious film to come out of Hollywood to that date, and for Ramon Novarro, his greatest success. Four years later, talkies arrived and Novarro's movie career died.

Though Novarro starred in a couple of musicals, his last major role in a movie was with Greta Garbo in *Mata Hari* (1932). In later years, he accepted cameo roles, mainly as a villain (*The Big Steal*, 1949).

EDWARD JAMES OLMOS

Actor
(1947–   )

Edward James Olmos was born in East Los Angeles, California, in 1947 to parents of Mexican descent, and he grew up in a poor neighborhood of mixed immigrants. Although he was adept at baseball, his interests turned to music and he formed a combo that enjoyed some success. He earned an associate degree in sociology at East Los Angeles City College and took some drama courses, which turned him on to acting.

He worked as a mover while trying to establish himself as an actor, winning some bit parts in television police action series and films. His major breakthrough came in *Zoot Suit*, a musical drama based on a trumped-up murder charge against some young Mexican-Americans in 1942. He appeared in several acclaimed theatrical versions and an adaptation of Zoot Suit film.

He went on to appear in the offbeat films *Wolfen* and *Blade Runner*, then starred in *The Ballad of Gregorio Cortez*, a movie based on a real-life Texas case. Olmos had appeared in some episodes of *Hill Street Blues* before being offered a regular role as a police lieutenant in *Miami Vice*. His lead role in *Stand and Deliver*, based on the life of a Bolivian-born computer genius who gives up his electronics career to teach in a delinquency-ridden East Los Angeles high school, won Olmos an Oscar nomination. He also has directed and produced such films as *Mí Familia* and *American Me*.

Although he has played a Greek Jewish boxer who fights to survive while in a Nazi concentration camp, primarily Olmos chooses Hispanic roles.

ANTHONY QUINN
Actor (1915–   )

Anthony Quinn was born in Chihuahua, Mexico, on April 21, 1915, the son of a Mexican mother and an Irish-Mexican father. After years of poverty and numerous odd jobs, Anthony broke into films in 1936. Despite marrying Katherine DeMille, the famous director's daughter, in 1937, Quinn spent nearly twenty years playing bit parts in movies. He was frequently cast as an Indian warrior.

Today, Quinn's film career has spanned almost half a century and includes over 150 films. He has played many notable larger-than-life figures, including Chief Crazy Horse in *They Died with Their Boots On*, Zapata in *Viva Zapata!*, Attila the Hun in *Attila*, Gauguin in *Lust for Life*, Quasimodo in *The Hunchback of Notre Dame*, the title role in *Barabbas*, the title role in *Zorba the Greek*, and Kublai Khan in *Marco the Magnificent*. He has been awarded two Oscars for best supporting actor, for Zapata in 1952 and also for Gauguin in 1956.

Quinn has appeared in numerous dramatic roles on television, and has held nine major exhibitions of his oil paintings, sculptures, and serigraphs. He is the author of the autobiographical *The Original Sin*, which was published in 1972. After bypass surgery in 1989, Quinn returned to Hollywood and making films. In 1994, he worked with costar Katharine Hepburn on the film *This Can't Be Love*.

ROBERT RODRIGUEZ
Screenwriter, Producer, Director
(1969–   )

"EL MARIACHI"

Young Robert Rodriguez has, on the strength of his early movie output, secured a two-year development and production deal at Columbia Pictures. This young talent from San Antonio, Texas, wrote and directed both the feature film *El Mariachi* and the short film *Bedhead*, which has won a number of awards.

The third oldest in a Catholic family of ten (five boys, five girls), Rodriguez showed an early interest in cartooning and filmmaking. Upon graduating from high school, he attended the University of Texas at Austin, intending to enroll in their film program. While there, he started a daily comic strip entitled *Los Hooligans*, featuring characters inspired by his younger siblings which ran for three years in the *Daily Texan* newspaper.

Rodriguez's rags-to-riches story began in 1991, when he chose to become a hospital research subject. "I checked myself into a research hospital to write the script and earn some money." He said he had a lot of free time to watch movies and write the script for *El Mariachi*, and earn $3,000.

"Except for the camera, everything else was ours," says Rodriguez when asked about the elements that went into the feature film *El Mariachi*. He wrote (with Carlos Gallardo), produced, and directed the film. "We had a school bus, a pit bull, a motorcycle, two bars and a ranch. So I wrote the script around these elements." He's not kidding—the whole film got made for $7,000. His most recent film, *Desperado*, solidified his reputation as one of Hollywood's hottest young filmmakers.

LINDA RONSTADT
Singer
(1946–)

Born in Tucson, Arizona, in 1946, Linda Ronstadt grew up in her hometown but her dreams of a career took her to Los Angeles at age 18. Three years later, she racked up her first hit song, "Different Drum," with the Stone Poney band backing her up on the recording.

It took nearly a decade after that for Linda to gain recognition as one of the best female vocalists of her time, her looks and natural charm merely enhancing a strong, versatile voice. Her career has been marked by a willingess to try various styles of music. When she recorded an album of Mexican songs in 1988, *Canciones de mi Padre*, she returned to her heritage, tapping music she had heard as a child at home.

Linda's father, Gilbert, was the brother of Luisa Ronstadt Espinel, a noted singer, dancer, and actress in the thirties who was a trained classical musician and a specialist in Hispanic folk music; she toured Spain, learning and later performing the songs and dances of Spanish country folk. Linda's grandfather, Frederico Ronstadt, had come to Tucson from Mexico as a young man, worked in railroading, and then became a successful manufacturer of wagons, buggies, saddles, and harnesses. He once founded a band, the Club Filharmonica, and toured the Southwest.

Wherever Linda Ronstadt's career takes her, she will carry with her a family tradition steeped in Hispanic musical lore, what she calls "a living memory of heartfelt experience."

THERESA SALDANA
Actress
(1954–   )

Versatile stage, film, and television actress Theresa Saldana starred as Rachel Scali, Tony's ever-understanding wife, in *The Commish*. Born in Brooklyn, New York, Saldana trained with famed acting coach Sanford Meisner. Her acting, dancing, and vocal talents kept her busy on the New York stage.

She made her feature film debut in Universal Pictures' *Nunzio*, followed by starring roles in such films as *I Wanna Hold Your Hand*; *Defiance*; *The Evil That Men Do*; *Home Movies*; and the critically acclaimed *Raging Bull*, as Robert De Niro's sister-in-law, Lenore La Motta.

In 1982, amidst a flourishing career, Saldana was near fatally stabbed by a deranged fan. This life-altering ordeal presented Saldana with an in-depth awareness of the suffering endured by victims of violent crimes, prompting her to form the nonprofit organization Victims for Victims, which is dedicated to helping crime victims and their families.

In 1984, Saldana starred in the NBC Movie of the Week *Victims for Victims: The Theresa Saldana Story*, for which she was honored by various organizations. She has since achieved recognition as one of the country's leading victims' rights advocates and public speakers and has received many awards, including a presidential commendation, for outstanding service on behalf of crime victims.

Theresa was thrilled to receive a 1994 Golden Globe nomination for Best Supporting Actress in *The Commish*. In September 1995, ABC commissioned three two-hour episodes of *The Commish* which aired in 1996, starring Michael Chiklis, Theresa Saldana, and Rod Steiger.

In February 1996 Theresa starred in an ABC Movie of the Week called *She Woke Up Pregnant*, in which she plays the role of the assistant district attorney (Doris).

SELENA
Singer
(1971–1995)

In death, Selena Quintanilla-Pérez became a symbol of the growing interest in Hispanic-based music and the marketability of its records and personalities. *People* magazine sold out several printings of its commemorative issue devoted to the Tejano star, and sales of her album soared in the wake of her murder and the trial and conviction of the woman who had built Selena's fan-club base.

She was born in Lake Jackson, Texas, to a father who was then a shipping clerk but had once been a singer himself. He recognized and encouraged his children's musical talent. He opened a Tex-Mex restaurant, where the three kids—Selena and her brother and sister—would perform. The restaurant failed and the trio toured South Texas to help pay family bills.

At 15, Selena won the Tejano Music Award for female vocalist of the year. Her recordings continued to draw attention and Selena earned a Grammy in 1994. Her concerts drew up to 80,000 people. Ironically, she had never learned any Spanish and had to speak lyrics phonetically. In dress and manner, Selena projected an increasingly sexy persona. She had married guitarist Chris Pérez, but even after the news was released, her fan base kept increasing. Living modestly near her family in Corpus Christi, Selena had developed a successful clothing and jewelry line. She was slated to become the first major crossover star from lively Tejano music to mainstream entertainment, but that was not to be.

MARTIN SHEEN

Actor
(1940–   )

Born in Dayton, Ohio, in 1940, Ramon Estevez left for New York City to pursue a theatrical career while a senior in high school and adopted the stage name Martin Sheen to avoid being limited to Latin roles. He had worked as a caddy and at first wanted to be a golfer, but an acting role in high school and some television talent show prizes turned him into an aspiring actor. He worked at numerous menial jobs and ate frequently at a Salvation Army soup kitchen while waiting for acting opportunities. He apprenticed briefly at the off-off-Broadway Living Theatre and Actor's Co-op, his only formal training.

Sheen's Broadway breakthrough came in a flop, *Never Live Over a Pretzel Factory*. But then he appeared in the critically acclaimed *The Subject Was Roses*. His career took off on television with *East Side, West Side* and an array of guest appearances on dramatic series. He also appeared in Joseph Papp Shakespearean productions. His film appearances include *Catch-22*, *Apocalypse Now*, *Gandhi*, *Badlands*, and *Wall Street*.

Sheen's children have followed in their dad's footsteps. Emilio Estevez and Charlie Sheen have taken impressive steps toward acting success; their brother Ramon and sister Renee have appeared in some films.

Their father has gained fame in recent years in another arena—that of social protestor. His deep sense of pacifism has brought numerous arrests for trespassing at a nuclear bomb test site and at nuclear plants.

RITCHIE VALENS

Singer, Songwriter
(1942–1959)

Rock music lovers are familiar with the songs of Ritchie Valens, even though his career was short-lived. Growing up in the barrios of Los Angeles, Valens knew early on that his guitar was his ticket out.

At seventeen, he signed a contract with a small record producer who changed the young singer's last name from Valenzuelas to Valens, making it easier for disc jockeys to pronounce. His first record, "Come On Let's Go," became a smash hit, making him the first Mexican-American rock star. Valens sang "La Bamba" in Spanish, though he did not speak the language of his ancestors. "La Bamba," based on a Mexican folk song, became his best-known song.

His short career ended tragically in February 1959, when he and two other rock-and-roll stars died in the crash of a chartered plane in Iowa. They had been on their way to a concert in North Dakota.

In 1988, a movie of Ritchie Valens's life entitled *La Bamba* was released, exposing a whole new generation to Ritchie's music.

MILITARY HEROES

A special thanks to the folks at the U.S. Army War College, Carlisle Barracks, Pennsylvania, and the Congressional Medal of Honor Society, Mt. Pleasant, South Carolina, for supplying much of the information contained in this chapter.

HERO STREET, U.S.A.

In Silvis, Illinois, just west of Chicago, stands a monument to eight heroes of Mexican-American descent who gave their lives in defense of this nation. The monument is a street once named Second Street, now renamed Hero Street U.S.A.

It is not much of a street in size, just one and a half blocks long. The street is muddy with rain in the spring, slick with snow in the winter. Joe Gomez (who earned a Silver Star), Peter Masias, Johnny Munos, Tony Pompa, Frank Sandoval, and Claro Soliz grew up together on this small street in a very close-knit environment working for the railroad, as did their fathers who came from Mexico years before. They went to war without hesitation, even though their streets were not paved and citizens of Silvis chose to ignore the docile, hard-working Mexicans on the edge of town. They never came back.

The men from the 22 families on this block who participated in World War II, Korea, and Vietnam totals 84. In World War II and Korea, 57 men went from this street. The two Sandoval families sent 13: 6 from one family; 7 from the other. Three Sandoval sons did not come back. This street reportedly contributed more men to military service in two wars—World War II and Korea—than any other place of comparable size in the United States. Hero Street U.S.A. stands alone in American military history.

STORIES OF HONOR

Hispanic-Americans have valiantly served our nation through all of its armed struggles. Patriotism, coupled with thoughts of improved opportunity after the guns stopped firing, have been the primary motivations. Either voluntarily or by conscription they entered every great American battle though constantly being denied equal opportunities at home. With unabashed pride and determination they rose to every challenge. Therefore, Hispanic patriotism must be considered uncommon valor.

As with so many Hispanic achievements, their heroism is often overlooked in history lessons. For example, during the Revolutionary War, when the American colonies were struggling to fend off the powerful British army, the king of Spain offered a hefty donation of 2 million pounds to the Revolutionary War effort. Moreover, although not acknowledged in many history books, Hispanics played a major role in defending the Gulf of Mexico and Mississippi River Valley against the British.

It is a little known fact that six Mexican-Texans fought and died with Colonel William Travis, Davey Crocket, and others while defending the Alamo on March 6, 1836. Those freedom fighters and other Hispanics opposed the rule of the Mexican government and supported the independence movement during the Texas War of Independence.

Approximately 9,900 Mexican-Americans fought in the Civil War, serving on both sides of the Mason-Dixon Line. For their service during the Civil War, Seaman Phillip Bazaar and Seaman John Ortego, were the first Hispanics to be awarded this country's highest military award - the Medal of Honor.

The Spanish-American war in Cuba saw Hispanics gallantly battle and ride as members of Theodore Roosevelt's "Rough Riders."

World War I and World War II once again featured Hispanics in the middle of the action. From scattered reports, the exact number of Hispanic-Americans in World War I is unknown. However, World War II engaged between 250,000 and 500,000

Hispanics. Thirteen won the Medal of Honor during the course of both wars.

President Harry Truman desegregated the armed forces in 1948. The Korean Conflict was the first conflict in which American troops fought side by side. Prior to that, Black Hispanic-Americans had been assigned to Black units while their White Hispanic cohorts were placed in segregated White units. Both were systematically prevented from sharing their Hispanic culture and language.

The Puerto Rican 65th Infantry Regiment, an all-Hispanic unit, earned the Presidential Unit Citation, a Meritorious Unit Commendation, and two Republic of Korea Unit Citations. Individuals received more than 200 awards for bravery and heroism. During the conflict, nine Hispanics received the Medal of Honor for acts of bravery.

The Vietnam era saw Hispanics, representing approximately four percent of the United States armed forces, serve their nation. Between 1961 and 1969, 8,016 soldiers from Arizona, California, Colorado, New Mexico, and Texas were killed. Of that number, more than 19 percent had Hispanic surnames. During the Vietnam era, 13 Hispanics were awarded the Medal of Honor.

In Libya, Grenada, Panama, and in the recent Persian Gulf crisis, Hispanics have proven again to be a credit to themselves, their ancestry, and our nation.

In the enlisted ranks today, Hispanics make up 4.6 percent of the Army, 6 percent of the Navy, 7.3 percent of the Marine Corps, 3.8 percent of the Air Force, and 4.6 percent of the Coast Guard. The officer component is a different picture. Hispanics compromise only 1.9 percent of Army officers, 2.4 percent of Navy, 2.4 percent of Marine Corps, 2 percent of the Air Force, and 1.7 percent of Coast Guard.

Hispanics served while others of better circumstances sought refuge in the Reserves and National Guard to escape the label "killed or missing in action." They served with memories of poor treatment, discrimination, and segregation, their culture under incessant attack for generations. They served knowing that the character and achievements of Hispanics, as a people, have been consistently disparaged.

They served with words "wetback" and "spic" ringing in their ears insulting their dignity. They served with misinterpreted, prejudiced disregard and negative historical stereotypical images of a lazy Mexican taking a never-ending siesta, a Puerto Rican gang member from the "West Side" of town, a Cuban drug smuggler, a terrorist fighting in the jungles of Central and South America, ilegal aliens, or the bandidos of the Alamo who killed John Wayne.

Time and again they returned home from the battlefield, knocking at the door of the land of opportunity to find limited answers. Perhaps, on this occasion, as they march in the ranks of heroes throughout the streets of America, somebody will be at home.

DOMINGO ARROYO
PFC, U.S. Marine Corps
(1971–1993)

Domingo Arroyo was born in Puerto Rico on March 9, 1971. He moved to the United States from Caguas, Puerto Rico, in the mid-1980s, graduating from the Elizabeth, New Jersey High School in 1989. He was described by relatives as an ambitious, athletic young man. A month after graduation, Domingo joined the United States Marine Corps.

As part of the 3rd Battalion, 11th Marine Regiment, based in Twenty-nine Palms, California, Arroyo was trained as a radio wireman. In December of 1992, his unit was sent to Somalia to aid in the distribution of food to the starving country.

On January 12, 1993, Arroyo was patrolling near Mogadishi Airport when his patrol was ambushed by Somali gunmen. Tragically, Arroyo became the first U.S. serviceman killed in Somalia.

Arroyo had planned on attending college when his tour of duty ended in April 1993. Flags in his hometown of Elizabeth were flown at half-staff for thirty days in his memory.

DAVID GLASGOW FARRAGUT
Admiral
(1801–1870)

The son of a Spanish sea captain who had come to America to help the colonists in their revolution against England and had remained, James Glasgow Farragut was born in Stony Point, Tennessee in 1801. Navy Captain David Porter adopted the eight-year-old Farragut after his mother died and James changed his first name in honor of his new dad, who would make him a midshipman.

Although he gained experience fighting British whalers in the War of 1812 and serving in such places as the Caribbean, he did not get to command a ship until 1824. Naval berths and promotions were hard to come by after the War of 1812. Farragut was married and living in Virginia when the Civil War broke out. Then a commander, he remained true to the Union, moved North and, late in life and career, made himself a legend.

He was chosen to lead a 17-ship attack on New Orleans from the South, sailed up the Mississippi through a barrage from two forts, overwhelmed a small Confederate squadron and forced the surrender of New Orleans. A year later, he ran two ships past Southern batteries to help Gen. U. S. Grant stem the flow of supplies to the South from the West.

In the Battle of Mobile Bay, there was not only fire from Fort Morgan but a field of submerged mines, then called torpedoes. As the ships faltered, he bellowed his now famous call, "Damn the torpedoes, full speed ahead!" Congress made Farragut an admiral and he was sent to Europe where he was lauded for his exploits.

HISPANIC CONGRESSIONAL
MEDAL OF HONOR RECIPIENTS

Navy Medal of Honor Winners in the Civil War

PHILLIP BAZAAR Ordinary Seaman, U.S. Navy

Born in Chile, South America. Citation: On board the U.S.S. *Santiago de Cuba* during the assault on Fort Fisher on January 15, 1865. As one of a boat crew detailed to one of the generals on shore, O. S. Bazaar bravely entered the fort in the assault and accompanied his party in carrying dispatches at the height of the battle.

JOHN ORETEGA Seaman, U.S. Navy

Born 1840 in Spain. Citation: On December 31, 1864, aboard the U.S.S. *Saratoga*, Seaman Oretega acted courageously during combat engagments with the enemy. Oretega was promoted to Acting Master's Mate.

Boxer Rebellion

FRANCE SILVA PFC, U.S. Marine Corps (1876–1951)

Born in Haywards, California, May 8, 1876. Citation: In the presence of the enemy during the action of Peking, China, June 28 to August 17, 1900. Throughout this period, Silva distinguished himself by meritorious conduct.

World War Two

LUCIAN ADAMS

Staff Sergeant, U.S. Army, 30th Inf., 3rd Infantry Division.
(1922–   )

Born October 26, 1922, in Port Arthur, Texas. Citation: For conspicuous gallantry and intrepidity at risk of life above and beyond the call of duty on October 28, 1944, near St. Die, France. When his company was stopped in its effort to drive through the Mortagne Forest to reopen the supply line to the isolated 3rd battalion, S/Sgt. Adams braved the concentrated fire of machineguns in a lone assault on a force of German troops. Although his company had progressed less than 10 yards and had lost 3 killed and 5 wounded, S/Sgt. Adams charged forward dodging from tree to tree firing a borrowed BAR from the hip. Despite intense machinegun fire which the enemy directed at him and rifle grenades which struck the trees over his head, S/Sgt. Adams made his way to within 10 yards of the closest machinegun and killed the gunner with a handgrenade. An enemy soldier threw grenades at him from a position only 10 yards distant; however, S/Sgt. Adams dispatched him with a single burst of BAR fire. Charging into the vortex of the enemy fire, he killed another machinegunner with a handgrenade and forced the surrender of 2 others. Although the remaining of the German group concentrated the full force of its automatic weapons fire in a desperate effort to knock him out, he proceeded through the woods to find and exterminate 5 more of the enemy. Finally, when the third German machinegun opened up on him at a range of 20 yards S/Sgt. Adams killed the gunner with BAR fire. In the course of the action, he personally killed 9 Germans, eliminated 3 enemy machineguns, vanquished a specialized force which was armed with automatic weapons and grenade launchers.

MARCARIO GARCIA

Staff Sergeant, U.S. Army,
22nd Inf., 4th Infantry
Division.
(1920–1972)

Sergeant Garcia was born: January 20, 1920, Villa de Castano, Mexico. He entered the service at Sugarland, Texas. Macario, as a squad leader of Company B, 22nd Infantry, 4th Infantry Division, on the 27th of November, 1944, outside the German town of Grosshau, made solo attacks on two enemy machinegun nests that had his unit pinned down. Although painfully wounded, he charged the emplacements, throwing grenades as he crawled forward. With his rifle, he killed six fleeing foes and captured 4 prisoners.

Sergeant Garcia continued fighting with his men until the objective was secured and only then did he permit himself to be removed for medical care.

Like other returning La Raza military heroes, Sergeant Garcia had one more "Battle" to overcome. One day after returning to his home town, he entered the Oasis Cafe, sat down, and ordered a cup of coffee. He was greeted by the owner with "We don't serve no Mexies in Here!" Macario replied, "If I'm good enough to fight your war for you, I'm good enough for you to serve a cup of coffee to." The proprietor grabbed Macario, but the combat trained Sergeant quickly reacted and dropped him with little effort.

Staff Sergeant Garcia was presented the Congressional Medal of Honor by President Harry S. Truman. He is buried at Houston National Cemetery, Houston, Texas.

HAROLD GONSALVES
PFC, 4th Battalion,
15th Marines, 6th Marine
Division.
(1926–1945)

Born in Alameda, California, January 28, 1926. Citation: For conspicuous gallantry and intrepidity at the risk of his life above and beyond the call of duty while serving as Acting Scout Sgt. with the 6th Marine Division, during action against enemy Japanese forces on Okinawa, April 15, 1945.

Undaunted by the powerfully organized opposition encountered during the fierce assault waged by his battalion against the enemy stronghold at Mount Yaetake, Pfc. Gonsalves repeatedly braved the terrific enemy bombardment to aid his forward observation team in directing well-placed artillery fire. When his commanding officer determined to move into the front lines in order to register a more effective bombardment in the enemy's defensive position, he unhesitatingly advanced uphill with the officer and another Marine despite a slashing barrage of enemy mortar and rifle fire. As they reached the front a Japanese grenade fell close to the group, instantly Pfc. Gonsalves dived on the deadly missile, absorbing the exploding charge in his body and thereby protecting the others from serious and perhaps fatal wounds. Stouthearted and indomitable, Pfc. Gonsalves readily yielded his own chances of survival that his fellow marines might carry on the relentless battle against a fanatic enemy and his cool decision, prompt action and valiant spirit of self-sacrifice in the face of certain death reflect the highest credit upon himself and the U.S. Naval Service.

Pfc. Harold Gonsalves is buried at Golden Gate National Cemetery, San Bruno, California.

David M. Gonzales

PFC, U.S. Army, 127th Inf.,
32nd Infantry Division.
(?–1945)

Born in Pacoima, Calif. Citation: He was pinned down with his company (at Villa Verde Trail, Luzon, Philippine Islands, April 25, 1945). As enemy fire swept the area, making any movement extremely hazardous. A 500-pound bomb smashed into the company's perimeter, burying five men with its explosion. Pfc. Gonzales, without hesitation, seized an entrenching tool and under a hail of fire, crawled 15 yards to his entombed comrades, where his commanding officer, who had also rushed forward, was beginning to dig the men out. Nearing his goal, he saw the officer struck and instantly killed by machinegun fire. Undismayed, he set to work swiftly and surely with his hands and the entrenching tool while enemy sniper and machinegun bullets struck all about him. He succeeded in digging one of the men out of the pile of rock and sand. To dig faster he stood up regardless of the greater danger from so exposing himself, he extricated a second man, and then another. As he completed the liberation of the third, he was hit and mortally wounded, but the comrades for whom he so gallantly gave his life were safely evacuated. Pfc. Gonzales's valiant and intrepid conduct exemplifies the highest tradition of the military service.

Pfc. David M. Gonzales is buried at Calvary Cemetery, Los Angeles, California.

SILVESTRE S. HERRERA

PFC, U.S. Army, Company E, 142nd Inf., 36th Infantry Division.
(1917–   )

Born July 17, 1917, in El Paso, Texas. Citation: He advanced with a platoon along a wooded road until stopped by heavy enemy machinegun fire (near Mertzwiller, France, March 15, 1945). As the rest of the unit took cover, he made a one-man frontal assault on a strongpoint and captured eight enemy soldiers. When the platoon resumed its advance and was subjected to fire from a second emplacement beyond an extensive minefield, Pfc. Herrera again moved forward, disregarding the danger of exploding mines to attack the position. He stepped on a mine and had both feet severed; but, despite intense pain and unchecked loss of blood, he pinned down the enemy with accurate rifle fire while a friendly squad captured the enemy gun by skirting the minefield and rushing in from the flank. The magnificent courage, extraordinary heroism, and willing self-sacrifice displayed by Pfc. Herrera resulted in the capture of two enemy strong-points and the taking of eight prisoners.

JOSE M. LOPEZ

Sergeant, U.S. Army, 23rd Inf., 2nd Infantry Division.

(1912–   )

Born June 1, 1912, in Mission, Texas. Citation: On his own initiative, he carried his heavy machinegun from company K's right flank to its left, in order to protect that flank which was in danger of being overrun by advancing enemy infantry supported by tanks (near Krinkelt, Belgium, December 17, 1944). Occupying a shallow hole offering no protection above his waist, he cut down a group of 10 Germans ignoring enemy fire from an advancing tank, he held his position and cut down 25 more enemy attempting to turn his flank. Glancing to his right, he saw a large group swarming in from the front. Although dazed and shaken from enemy artillery fire, he realized that his position would be outflanked. Again, alone, he carried his machinegun to a position to the right rear of the sector; enemy tanks and infantry were forcing a withdrawal. Blown over backward by the concussion of enemy fire, he immediately reset his gun and continued his fire. Singlehanded he held off the German horde until he was satisfied his company had effected its retirement. Again he loaded his gun on his back and in a hail of small-arms fire he ran to a point where a few of his comrades were attempting to set up another defense against the onrushing enemy. He fired from this position until his ammunition was exhausted. Still carrying his gun, he fell back with his small group to Krinkelt. Sgt. Lopez's gallantry and intrepidity, on seemingly suicidal missions in which he killed at least 100 of the enemy.

7th Div.

JOE P. MARTINEZ

Private, U.S. Army,
Company K,
32nd Inf., 7th Infantry
Division.
(1920–1943)

Born July 27, 1920, in Taos, New Mexico. Citation: For conspicuous gallantry and intrepidity above and beyond the call of duty in action with the enemy (On Attu, Aleutians, May 26, 1943). Over a period of several days, repeated efforts to drive the enemy from a key defensive position high in the snow covered precipitous mountains between East Arm Holtz Bay and Chichagof Harbor had failed. On May 26, 1943, troop dispositions were readjusted and a trial coordinated attack on this position by a reinforced battalion was launched. Initially successful, the attack hesitated. In the face of severe hostile machinegun, rifle, and mortar fire, Pvt. Martinez, an automatic rifleman, rose to his feet and resumed his advance. Occasionally he stopped to urge his comrades on. His example inspired others to follow. After a most difficult climb, he eliminated resistance from part of the enemy position by BAR fire and handgrenades, thus assisting the advance of other attacking elements. This success partially completed the action. The main Holtz-Chichagof Pass rose about 150 feet higher, flanked by steep rocky ridges and reached by a snow-filled defile. Passage was barred by enemy fire from either flank and from tiers of snow trenches in front. Despite these obstacles, and knowing of their existence, Pvt. Martinez again led the troops on and up, personally silencing several trenches with BAR fire and ultimately reaching the pass itself. Here just below the rim of the pass, Pvt. Martinez encountered a final enemy-occupied trench and was mortally wounded while firing into it. However, due to his action organized hostile resistance ended on the island.

Joe P. Martinez is buried at Ault Cemetery, Ault, Colorado.

MANUEL
PEREZ, JR.
PFC, U.S. Army, Company A,
511th Parachute Inf.,
11th Airborne Division.
(1923–1945)

Born March 3, 1923 in Oklahoma City, OK. Citation: He was scout for Company A, which had destroyed 11 of 12 pillboxes in a strongly fortified sector defending the approach to enemy-held Fort William McKinley on Luzon, Philippine Islands (February 13, 1945). In the reduction of these pillboxes, he killed 5 Japanese in the open and blasted others in pillboxes with grenades. Realizing the urgent need for taking the last emplacement, which contained 2 twin-mount .50-caliber machineguns, he took a circuitous route to within 20 yards of position, killing 4 of the enemy in his advance. He threw a grenade into the pillbox, and, as the crew started withdrawing through a tunnel just to the rear of the emplacement, shot and killed 4 before exhausting his clip. He had reloaded and killed 4 more when an escaping Japanese threw his rifle with fixed bayonet at him. In warding off this thrust, his own rifle was knocked to the ground. Seizing the Jap rifle, he continued firing, killing 2 more of the enemy. He rushed the remaining Japanese, where he bayoneted the 1 surviving hostile soldier. Singlehandedly, he killed 18 of the enemy in neutralizing the position that had held up the advance of his entire company. Through his courageous determination and heroic disregard of grave danger, Pfc. Perez made possible the successful advance of his unit toward a valuable objective and provided a lasting inspiration for his comrades.

Pfc. Manuel Perez is buried at Fairlawn Cemetery, Oklahoma City.

CLETO RODRIGUEZ
Tech/Sgt., U.S. Army, Company B, 148th Inf., 27th Infantry Division.

Born in Marcos, Texas. Citation: He was an automatic rifleman when his unit attacked the strongly defended Paco Railroad Station during the battle for Manila, Philippine Is. While making a frontal assault across an open field, his platoon was halted 100 yards from the station by intense enemy fire. On his own initiative, he left the platoon, accompanied by a comrade, and continued forward to a house 60 yards from the objective. Although under constant enemy observation, the 2 men remained in this position for an hour, firing at targets of opportunity, killing more than 35 hostile soldiers and wounding many more. Moving closer to the station and discovering a group of Japanese replacements attempting to reach pillboxes, they opened heavy fire, killing more than 40 and stopped all subsequent attempts to man the emplacements. Enemy fire became more intense as they advanced to within 20 yards of the station. Then, covered by his companion, Rodriguez boldly moved up to the building and threw grenades through a doorway killing 7 Japanese, destroying a 20-mm gun. With their ammunition running low, they started to return to their lines, during this movement, his companion was killed. In 2½ hours of fierce fighting the intrepid team killed more than 82 Japanese, completely disorganized their defense, and paved the way for the subsequent defeat of the enemy at this strongpoint. Two days later, Rodriguez again enabled his comrades to advance when he singlehandedly killed 6 Japanese and destroyed a wellplaced 20-mm gun.

Alejandro R. RENTERIA RUIZ

PFC, U.S. Army, 165th Inf.,
27th Infantry Division.

Born in Loving, New Mexico. Citation: When his unit was stopped by a skillfully camouflaged enemy pillbox (Okinawa, April 28, 1945), he displayed conspicuous gallantry and intrepidity above and beyond the call of duty. His squad, suddenly brought under a hail of machinegun fire and a vicious grenade attack, was pinned down. Jumping to his feet, Pfc. Ruiz seized an automatic rifle and lunged through the flying grenades and rifle and automatic fire for the top of the emplacement. When an enemy soldier charged him, his rifle jammed. Undaunted, Pfc. Ruiz whirled on his assailant and clubbed him down. Then he ran back through bullets and grenades, seized more ammunition and another automatic rifle, and again made for the pillbox. Enemy fire now was concentrated on him, but he charged on, miraculously reaching the position, and in plain view he climbed to the top. Leaping from 1 opening to another, he sent burst after burst into the pillbox, killing 12 of the enemy and completely destroying the position. Pfc. Ruiz's heroic conduct, in the face of overwhelming odds, saved the lives of many comrades and eliminated an obstacle that would have checked his unit's advance.

I'M HIT...BUT I HAVE TO KEEP FIRING!

3ʳᵈ INF. DIV.

JOSE F. VALDEZ
PFC, U.S. Army,
3rd Infantry Division.

Born in Governador, New Mexico. Citation: He was on outpost duty (near Rosenkrantz, France, January 25, 1945) with 5 others when the enemy counterattacked with overwhelming strength. From his position near some woods 500 yards beyond the American lines he observed a hostile tank about 75 yards away, and raked it with automatic rifle fire until it withdrew. Soon afterward he saw 3 Germans stealthily approaching through the woods. Scorning cover as the enemy soldiers opened up with heavy automatic weapons fire from a range of 30 yards, he engaged in a fire fight with the attackers until he had killed all 3. The enemy quickly launched an attack with 2 full companies of infantrymen, blasting the patrol with murderous concentrations of automatic and rifle fire and beginning an encircling movement which forced the patrol leader to order a withdrawal. Despite the terrible odds, Pfc. Valdez immediately volunteered to cover the maneuver, and as the patrol 1 by 1 plunged through a hail of bullets toward the American Lines, he fired bursts into the swarming enemy. Three of his companions were wounded in their dash for safety and he was struck by a bullet that entered his stomach and, passing through his body. Overcoming agonizing pain, he regained control of himself and resumed his firing position, delivering a protective screen of bullets until all others of the patrol were safe. By field telephone he called for artillery and mortar fire on the Germans and corrected the range until he had shells falling within 50 yards of his position. For 15 minutes he refused to be dislodged by more than 200 of the enemy; then, seeing that the barrage had broken the counterattack, he dragged himself back to his own lines. He died later as a result of his wounds.

Pfc. Valdez is buried at Sante Fe National Cemetery, New Mexico.

YSMAEL R. VILLEGAS

Staff Sergeant,
U.S. Army, 127th Inf.,
32nd Infantry Division.

Born in Casa Blanca, California. Citation: He was a squad leader when his unit, in a forward position (Villa Verde Trail, Luzon, Philippine Islands, March 20, 1945), clashed with an enemy strongly entrenched in connected caves and foxholes on commanding ground. He moved boldly from man to man, in the face of bursting grenades and demolition charges, through heavy machinegun and rifle fire, to bolster the spirit of his comrades. Inspired by his gallantry, his men pressed forward to the crest of the hill. Numerous enemy riflemen, refusing to flee, continued firing from their foxholes. S/Sgt. Villegas, with complete disregard for his own safety and the bullets which kicked up the dirt at his feet, charged an enemy position, and firing at point-blank range killed the Japanese in a foxhole. He rushed a second foxhole while bullets missed him by inches, and killed 1 more of the enemy. In rapid succession he charged a third, a fourth, a fifth foxhole, each time destroying the enemy within. The fire against him increased in intensity, but he pressed onward to attack a sixth position, as he neared his goal, he was hit and killed by enemy fire. His men were inspired to attack and sweep the enemy from the field.

S/Sgt. Ysmael R. Villegas is buried at Riverside National Cemetery, Riverside, California.

Korean War

REGINALD B. DESIDERIO

Captain, U.S. Army,
Commanding Officer,
Company E, 27th Inf. Reg.,
25th Inf. Division.
(1918–   )

Captain Desiderio was born September 12, 1918, in Clairton, Pennsylvania. Citation: Capt. Desiderio distinguished himself by conspicuous gallantry and intrepidity at the repeated risk of his life above and beyond the call of duty. His company was given the mission of defending the command post of a task force against an enemy breakthrough (near Ipsok, Korea, November 27, 1950). After personal reconnaissance during darkness and under intense enemy fire, he placed his men in defensive positions to repel an attack. Early in the action he was wounded, but refused evacuation and despite enemy fire continued to move among his men checking their positions and making sure that each element was prepared to receive the next attack. Again wounded, he continued to direct his men. By his inspiring leadership he encouraged them to hold their position. In the subsequent fighting when the fanatical enemy succeeded in penetrating the position, he personally charged them with carbine, rifle and grenades, inflicting many casualties until he himself was mortally wounded. His men, spurred on by his intrepid example, repelled this final attack. Capt. Desiderio's heroic leadership, courageous and loyal devotion to duty, and his complete disregard for personal safety reflect the highest honor on him and are in keeping with the esteemed traditions of the U.S. Army.

FERNANDO LUIS GARCIA

PFC, U.S. Marine Corps,
Co. I, 3rd Bn., 5th Marines,
1st Marine Division.
(1929–1952)

Born in Utuado, Puerto Rico, October 14, 1929. Citation: For conspicuous gallantry and intrepidity at the risk of his life above and beyond the call of duty while serving as a member of Company I, in action against enemy aggressor forces (Korea). While participating in the defense of a combat outpost located more than 1 mile forward of the main line of resistance during a savage night attack by a fanatical enemy force employing grenades, mortars, and artillery, Pfc. Garcia, although suffering painful wounds, moved through the intense hail of hostile fire to a supply point to secure more handgrenades. Quick to act when a hostile grenade landed nearby, endangering the life of another marine, as well as his own, he unhesitatingly chose to sacrifice himself and immediately threw his body upon the deadly missile, receiving the full impact of the explosion. His great personal valor and cool decision in the face of almost certain death sustain and enhance the finest traditions of the U.S. Naval Service. He gallantly gave his life for his country.

Pfc. Fernando Luis Garcia is buried at Puerto Rico National Cemetery, Bayamon, Puerto Rico.

EDWARD
GOMEZ
PFC, U.S. Marine Corps.
2nd Bn., 1st Marines,
1st Marine Division.
(1932–1951)

Born in Omaha, Nebraska, August 10, 1932. Citation: For conspicuous gallantry and intrepidity at the risk of his life above and beyond the call of duty while serving as an ammunition bearer in Company E, in action against enemy aggressor forces (Hill 749, Korea). Boldly advancing with his squad in support of a group of riflemen assaulting a series of strongly fortified and bitterly defended hostile positions on Hill 749, Pfc. Gomez consistently exposed himself to the withering barrage to keep his machinegun supplied with ammunition during the drive forward to seize the objective. As his squad deployed to meet an imminent counterattack, he voluntarily moved down an abandoned trench to search for a new location for the gun and, when a hostile grenade landed between himself and his weapon, shouted a warning to those around him as he grasped the activated charge in his hand determined to save his comrades, he unhesitatingly chose to sacrifice himself and, diving into the ditch with the deadly missile, absorbed the shattering violence of the explosion in his body. By his stouthearted courage, incomparable valor, and decisive spirit of self-sacrifice, Pfc. Gomez inspired the others to heroic efforts in subsequently repelling the outnumbering foe, and his valiant conduct throughout sustained and enhanced the finest traditions of the U.S. Naval Service. He gallantly gave his life for his country.

Pfc. Edward Gomez is buried at St. Mary's Cemetery, Omaha, Nebraska.

AMBROSIO GUILLEN

Staff Sergeant,
U.S. Marine Corps,
2nd Bn., 7th Marines,
1st Marine Division.
(1929–1953)

Born in La Junta, Colorado, December 7, 1929. Citation: For conspicuous gallantry and intrepidity at the risk of his life above and beyond the call of duty while serving as a platoon sergeant of Company F in action against enemy agressor forces (Near Songuch-on, Korea, July 25, 1953). Participating in the defense of an outpost forward of the main line of resistance, S/Sgt. Guillen maneuvered his platoon over unfamiliar terrain in the face of hostile fire and placed his men in fighting positions. With his unit pinned down when the outpost was attacked under cover of darkness by an estimated force of 3 battalions supported by mortar and artillery fire, he deliberately exposed himself to the heavy barrage and attacks to direct his men in defending their positions and personally supervise the treatment and evacuation of the wounded. Inspired by his leadership, the platoon quickly rallied and engaged the enemy in fierce hand-to-hand combat. Although critically wounded during the course of the battle, S/Sgt. Guillen refused medical aid and continued to direct his men throughout the remainder of the engagement until the enemy was defeated and thrown into disorderly retreat. Succumbing to his wounds within a few hours, S/Sgt. Guillen, by his outstanding courage and indomitable fighting spirit, was directly responsible for the success of his platoon in repelling a numerically superior enemy force.

S/Sgt. Ambrosio Guillen is buried at Ft. Bliss National Cemetery, Ft. Bliss, Texas.

187TH AIRBORN
REGT. COMBAT
TEAM

RODOLFO P. HERNANDEZ

Corporal, U.S. Army,
Company G., 187th Airborne
Regimental Combat Team.
(1931–)

Born in Colton, California, April 14, 1931. Citation: Cpl. Hernandez, a member of Company G, distinguished himself by conspicuous gallantry and intrepidity above and beyond the call of duty in action against the enemy (near Wonton-ni, Korea, May 31, 1951). His platoon, in defensive positions of hill 420, came under ruthless attack by a numerically superior and fanatical hostile force, accompanied by heavy artillery, mortar, and machinegun fire which inflicted numerous casualties on the platoon. His comrades were forced to withdraw due to lack of ammunition but Cpl. Hernandez, although wounded in an exchange of grenades, continued to deliver deadly fire into the ranks of the onrushing assailants until a ruptured cartridge rendered his rifle inoperative. Immediately leaving his position, Cpl. Hernandez rushed the enemy armed only with rifle and bayonet. Fearlessly engaging the foe, he killed 6 of the enemy before falling unconscious from grenade, bayonet, and bullet wounds but his heroic action momentarily halted the enemy advance and enabled his unit to counterattack and retake the lost ground. The indomitable fighting spirit, outstanding courage, and tenacious devotion to duty clearly demonstrated by Cpl. Hernandez reflect the highest credit upon himself, the infantry, and the U.S. Army.

BALDOMERO LOPEZ

1st Lieutenant,
U.S. Marines Corps,
Company A, 1st Bn.,
5th Marines,
1st Marine Division.
(1925–1950)

Born in Tampa, Florida, August 23, 1925. Citation: For conspicuous gallantry and intrepidity at the risk of his life above and beyond the call of duty as a rifle platoon commander of Company A, in action against enemy aggressor forces (during Inchon invasion in Korea, September 15, 1950). With his platoon 1st Lt. Lopez was engaged in the reduction of immediate enemy beach defenses after landing with the assault waves. Exposing himself to hostile fire, he moved forward alongside a bunker and prepared to throw a handgrenade into the next pillbox whose fire was pinning down that sector of the beach. Taken under fire by an enemy automatic weapon and hit in the right shoulder and chest as he lifted his arm to throw, he fell backward and dropped the deadly missile. After a moment, he turned and dragged his body forward in an effort to retrieve the grenade and throw it. In critical condition from pain and loss of blood, and unable to grasp the handgrenade firmly enough to hurl it, he chose to sacrifice himself rather than endanger the lives of his men and, with a sweeping motion of his wounded right arm, cradled the grenade under him and absorbed the full impact of the explosion. His exceptional courage, fortitude, and devotion to duty reflect the highest credit upon 1st Lt. Lopez and the U.S. Naval Service. He gallantly gave his life for his country.

Lt. Baldomero Lopez is buried at Centro Asturiano Memorial Park, Tampa, Florida.

BENITO
MARTINEZ
Corporal, U.S. Army,
Co. 1, 27th Inf. Regt.,
25th Infantry Division.
(1931–1952)

Born in Fort Hancock, Texas, March 21, 1931. Citation: Cpl. Martinez, a machine gunner with Company A, distinguished himself by conspicuous gallantry and outstanding courage above and beyond the call of duty in action against the enemy (near Satae-ri, Korea, September 5, 1952). While manning a listening post forward of the main line of resistance, his position was attacked by a hostile force of reinforced company strength in bitter fighting which ensued, the enemy infiltrated the defense perimeter and, realizing that encirclement was imminent, Cpl. Martinez elected to remain at his post in an attempt to stem the onslaught. In a daring defense, he raked the attacking troops with crippling fire, inflicting numerous casualties. Although contacted by sound power phone several times, he insisted that no attempt be made to rescue him because of the danger involved. Soon thereafter, the hostile forces rushed the emplacement, forcing him to make a limited withdrawal with only an automatic rifle and pistol to defend himself. After a courageous 6-hour stand and shortly before dawn, he called in for the last time, stating that the enemy was converging on his position. His magnificent stand enabled friendly elements to reorganize, attack, and regain the key terrain. Cpl. Martinez's incredible valor and supreme sacrifice reflect lasting glory upon himself and are in keeping with the honored traditions of the military service.

Cpl. Benito Martinez is buried at Ft. Hancock Cemetery, Ft. Hancock, Texas.

EUGENE ARNOLD OBREGON

PFC, U.S. Marine Corps,
3rd Bn., 5th Marines,
1st Marine Division.
(1930–1950)

Born in Los Angeles, California, November 12, 1930. Citation: For conspicuous gallantry and intrepidity at the risk of his life above and beyond the call of duty while serving with Company G, in action against enemy aggressor forces (Seoul, Korea). While serving as an ammunition carrier of a machinegun squad in a marine rifle company which was temporarily pinned down by hostile fire, Pfc. Obregon observed a fellow marine fall wounded in the line of fire. Armed only with a pistol, he unhesitatingly dashed from his covered position to the side of the casualty. Firing his pistol with 1 hand as he ran, he grasped his comrade by the arm with his other hand and, despite the great peril to himself dragged him to the side of the road. Still under enemy fire, he was bandaging the man's wounds when hostile troops of approximately platoon strength began advancing toward his position. Quickly seizing the wounded marine's carbine, he placed his own body as a shield in front of him and lay their firing accurately and effectively into the hostile group until he himself was fatally wounded by enemy machinegun fire. By his courageous fighting spirit, fortitude, and loyal devotion to duty, Pfc. Obregon enabled his fellow marines to rescue the wounded man and aided essentially in repelling the attack, thereby sustaining and enhancing the highest traditions of the U.S. Naval Service. He gallantly gave his life for his country.

Pfc. Eugene Arnold Obregon is buried at Calvary Cemetery, Los Angeles, California.

JOSEPH C. RODRIGUEZ

Sergeant, U.S. Army,
17th Inf. Regt.,
7th Infantry Division.
(1928–   )

Born in San Bernandino, California, November 14, 1928. Citation: Sgt. Rodriguez, distinguished himself by conspicuous gallantry and intrepidity at the risk of his life above and beyond the call of duty in action against an armed enemy of the United Nations (near Munye-ri, Korea, May 21, 1951). Sgt. Rodriguez, an assistant squad leader of the 2nd Platoon, was participating in an attack against a fanatical hostile force occupying well-fortified positions on rugged commanding terrain, when his squad's advance was halted within approximately 60 yards by a withering barrage of automatic weapons and small-arms fire from 5 emplacements directly to the front and right and left flanks, together with grenades which the enemy rolled down the hill toward the advancing troops. Fully aware of the odds against him, Sgt. Rodriguez leaped to his feet, dashed 60 yards up the fire-swept slope, and after lobbing grenades into the first foxhole with deadly accuracy, ran around the left flank, silenced an automatic weapon with 2 grenades and continued his whirlwind assault to the top of the peak, wiping out 2 more foxholes and then, reaching the right flank, he tossed grenades into the remaining emplacement, destroying the gun and annihilating its crew. Sgt. Rodriguez's intrepid actions exacted a toll of 15 enemy dead and, as a result of his incredible display of valor, the defense of the opposition was broken, and the enemy routed, and the strategic strongpoint secured.

Vietnam War

ROY P. BENAVIDEZ

Master Sergeant,
Detachment B-56,
5th Special Forces Group,
Republic of Vietnam.
(1935–   )

Born August 5, 1935 in Cuero, Texas, Sgt. Benavidez distinguished himself by a series of daring and extremely valorous actions west of Loc Ninh, Vietnam. On the morning of May 2, 1968, a 12-man Special Forces recon team were airlifted by helicopters to a dense jungle area to gather intelligence information on reported heavy enemy activity. Shortly after landing, the team met heavy enemy resistance and requested emergency extraction, 3 helicopters arrived at their position, but had to abort rescue attempts due to intense enemy ground fire, and returned to base with dead and wounded crewmembers. When a fresh flight of helicopter prepared for a second rescue attempt, Sgt. Benavidez volunteered to assist. Arriving at the site, he jumped from the hovering helicopter, and ran through withering small arms fire to the crippled team. Prior to reaching them he was wounded in his right leg, face, and head. Despite these painful injuries, he took charge, repositioning the team and directing their fire to facilitate the landing of an aircraft, and the loading of the casualties. He then threw smoke cannisters to direct other aircraft to the team's position. In later action at the site, he was twice more wounded. Sgt. Benavidez mustered his strength and called in gunships and fighter bombers to suppress the growing enemy fire. While giving first aid to the wounded, he was hit again, but he continued ferrying others to the helicopters. He made one final sweep of the perimeter to collect classified material, and to bring in the remaining wounded. Only then, in extremely serious condition from numerous wounds and loss of blood, did he allow himself to be pulled into the extration aircraft. He ended up killing at least 3 of the enemy, while saving at least eight comrades.

EMILIO A. DE LA GARZA

Lance Corporal, U.S. Marines,
2nd Bn., 1st Marine Division.
(1949–1970)

Born in East Chicago, Indiana, June 23, 1949. Citation: For conspicuous gallantry and intrepidity at the risk of his life above and beyond the call of duty while serving as a machine gunner with Company E. Returning with his squad from a night ambush operation (near Da Nang, Republic of Vietnam, April 11, 1970) L/Cpl. De La Garza joined his platoon commander and another marine in searching for 2 enemy soldiers who had been observed fleeing for cover toward a small pond. Moments later, he located 1 of the enemy soldiers hiding among the reeds and brush. As the 3 marines attempted to remove the resisting soldier from the pond, L/Cpl. De La Garza observed him pull the pin on a grenade. Shouting a warning, L/Cpl. De La Garza placed himself between the other 2 marines and the ensuing blast from the grenade, thereby saving the lives of his comrades at the sacrifice of his life. By his prompt and decisive action, and his great personal valor in the face of almost certain death, L/Cpl. De La Garza upheld and further enhanced the finest traditions of the Marine Corps and the U.S. Naval Service.

L/Cpl. De La Garza is buried at St. John's Cemetery, Hammond, Indiana.

RALPH E. DIAS

PFC, U.S. Marine Corps,
Co. D., 1st Bn.,
7th Marines,
1st Marine Division.
(1950–1969)

Born July 15, 1950, in Shelocta, Indiana Co., Pennsylvania. Citation: As a member of a reaction force which was pinned down by enemy fire while assisting a platoon in the same circumstance (Que Son Mountains, Republic of Vietnam, November 12, 1969), Pfc. Dias, observing that both units were sustaining casualties, initiated an aggressive assault against an enemy machinegun bunker which was the principal source of hostile fire. Severely wounded by enemy snipers while charging across the open area, he pulled himself to the shelter of a nearby rock. Braving enemy fire for a second time, Pfc. Dias was again wounded. Unable to walk, he crawled 15 meters to the protection of a rock located near his objective and, repeatedly exposing himself to intense hostile fire, unsuccessfully threw several handgrenades at the machinegun emplacement. Still determined to destroy the emplacement, Pfc. Dias again moved into the open and was wounded a third time by sniper fire. As he threw a last grenade which destroyed the enemy position, he was mortally wounded by another enemy round. Pfc. Dias's indomitable courage, dynamic initiative, and selfless devotion to duty upheld the highest traditions of the Marine Corps and the U.S. Naval Service. He gallantly gave his life in the service of his country.

Pfc. Ralph E. Dias is buried at Oakdale Cemetery, Leetonia, Ohio.

Daniel Fernandez

**Specialist 4th Class,
U.S. Army, 1st Bn.,
5th Inf., 25th Inf. Division.
(1944–1966)**

Born in Albuquerque, New Mexico, June 30, 1944. Citation: For conspicuous gallantry and intrepidity at the risk of his life above and beyond the call of duty. Sp4c. Fernandez demonstrated indomitable courage when the patrol was ambushed (Cu Chi, Hau Nghia Province, Rep. of Vietnam) by a Viet Cong rifle company and driven back by the intense enemy automatic weapons fire before it could evacuate an American soldier who had been wounded in the Viet Cong attack. Sp4c. Fernandez, a sergeant and 2 other volunteers immediately fought their way through devastating fire and exploding grenades to reach the fallen soldier. Upon reaching their fallen comrade the sergeant was struck in the knee by machinegun fire and immobilized. Sp4c. Fernandez took charge, rallied the left flank of his patrol and began to assist in the recovery of the wounded sergeant. While first aid was being administered to the wounded man, a sudden increase in the accuracy and intensity of enemy fire forced the volunteer group to take cover. As they did, an enemy grenade landed in the midst of the group, although some men did not see it. Realizing there was no time for the wounded sergeant or the other men to protect themselves from the grenade blast, Sp4c Fernandez vaulted over the wounded sergeant and threw himself on the grenade as it exploded, saving the lives of his 4 comrades at the sacrifice of his life.

Sp4c. Daniel Fernandez is buried at Santa Fe National Cemetery, Santa Fe, New Mexico.

ALFREDO GONZALEZ

Sergeant, U.S. Marine Corps,
Company A, 1st Bn.,
1st Marines,
1st Marine Div. (1946–1969)

Born in Edinburg, Texas, May 23, 1946. Citation: While serving as platoon commander on January 31, 1968, during the initial phase of Operation Hue City, Sgt. Gonzalez's unit was formed as a reaction force and deployed to Hue to relieve the pressure on the beleaguered city. While moving by truck convoy along Route #1, near the village of Lang Van Lrong, the marines received a heavy volume of enemy fire. Sgt. Gonzalez aggressively maneuvered the marines in his platoon, and directed their fire until the area was cleared of snipers. Immediately after crossing a river south of Hue, the column was again hit by intense enemy fire. One of the marines on top of a tank was wounded and fell to the ground in an exposed position. With complete disregard for his safety, Sgt. Gonzalez ran through the fire-swept area to the assistance of his injured comrade. He lifted him up and though receiving fragmentation wounds during the rescue, he carried the wounded marine to a covered position for treatment. Due to the increased volume and accuracy of enemy fire from a fortified machinegun bunker on the side of the road, the company was temporarily halted. Realizing the gravity of the situation, Sgt. Gonzalez exposed himself to the enemy fire and moved his platoon along the east side of a bordering rice paddy to a dike directly across from the bunker. Though fully aware of the danger involved, he moved to the fire-swept road and destroyed the hostile position with handgrenades. Although seriously wounded again on February 3, he steadfastly refused medical treatment and continued to supervise his men and lead the attack. On February 4, the enemy had again pinned the company down, inflicting heavy casualties with automatic weapons and rocket fire. Sgt. Gonzalez, utilizing a number of light antitank assault weapons, fearlessly moved from position to position firing numerous rounds at the heavily fortified enemy emplacements. He successfully knocked out a rocket position and suppressed much of the enemy fire before falling mortally wounded. The heroism, courage, and dynamic leadership displayed by Sgt. Gonzalez reflected great credit upon himself and the Marine Corps, and were in keeping with the highest traditions of the U.S. Naval Service. He gallantly gave his life for his country.

Sgt. Gonzalez is buried in Hillcrest Cemetery, Edingburg, Texas.

JOSE FRANCISCO JIMENEZ

Lance Corporal,
U.S. Marine Corps, 3rd Bn.,
7th Marines, 1st Marine
Division.
(1946–1969)

Born in Mexico City, Mexico, March 20, 1946. Citation: For conspicuous gallantry and intrepidity at the risk of his life above and beyond the call of duty while serving as a fire team leader with Company K, in operation against the enemy (Quang Nam Province, Rep. of Vietnam, August 28, 1969). L/Cpl. Jimenez's unit came under heavy attack by North Vietnamese soldiers concealed in well camouflaged emplacements. L/Cpl. Jimenez reacted by seizing the initiative and plunging forward toward the enemy positions. He personally destroyed several enemy personnel and silenced an antiaircraft weapon. Shouting encouragement to his companions, L/Cpl. Jimenez continued his aggressive forward movement. He slowly maneuvered to within 10 feet of hostile soldiers who were firing automatic weapons from a trench and, in the face of vicious enemy fire, destroyed the position. Although he was by now the target of concentrated fire from hostile gunners intent upon halting his assault, L/Cpl. Jimenez continued to press forward. As he moved to attack another enemy soldier, he was mortally wounded. L/Cpl. Jimenez's indomitable courage, aggressive fighting spirit and unfaltering devotion to duty upheld the highest traditions of the Marine Corps and of the U.S. Naval Service.

L/Cpl. Joe Francisco Jimenez is buried at Morelia Cemetery, Michoacan, Mexico.

MIGUEL KEITH

Lance Corporal,
U.S. Marine Corps,
III Marine Amphibious Force.
(1951–1970)

Born in San Antonio, Texas, June 2, 1951. Citation: For conspicuous gallantry and intrepidity at the risk of his life above and beyond the call of duty while serving as a machine gunner with Combined Action Platoon 1-3-2 (Quang Ngai Province, Rep. of Vietnam, May 8, 1970). During the early morning L/Cpl. Keith was seriously wounded when his platoon was subjected to a heavy ground attack by a greatly outnumbering enemy force. Despite his painful wounds, he ran across the fire-swept terrain to check the security of vital defensive positions and then, while completely exposed to view, proceeded to deliver a hail of devastating machinegun fire against the enemy. Determined to stop 5 of the enemy soldiers approaching the command post, he rushed forward, firing as he advanced. He succeeded in disposing of 3 of the attackers and in dispersing the remaining 2. At this point, a grenade detonated near L/Cpl. Keith, knocking him to the ground and inflicting further severe wounds. Fighting pain and weakness from loss of blood, he again braved the concentrated hostile fire to charge an estimated 25 enemy soldiers who were massing to attack. The vigor of his assault and his well placed fire eliminated 4 of the enemy soldiers while the remainder fled for cover. During this valiant effort, he was mortally wounded by an enemy soldier. By his courageous and inspiring performance in the face of almost overwhelming odds, L/Cpl. Keith contributed in large measure to the success of his platoon in routing a numerically superior enemy force.

L/Cpl. Miguel Keith is buried at Forest Lawn Cemetery, Omaha, Nebraska.

CARLOS JAMES LOZADA

PFC, U.S. Army, 2nd Bn., 503rd Inf., 173rd Airborne Brigade.
(1946–1967)

Born in Caguas, Puerto Rico, September 6, 1946. Citation: For conspicuous gallantry and intrepidity in action at the risk of his life above and beyond the call of duty. Pfc. Lozada, distinguished himself in the battle of Dak To (Vietnam). While serving as a machine gunner with Company A, Pfc. Lozada was part of a 4-man early warning outpost, located 35 meters from his company's lines. At 1400 hour a North Vietnamese Army company rapidly approached the outpost along a well defined trail. Pfc. Lozada alerted his comrades and commenced firing at the enemy who were within 10 meters of the outpost. His heavy and accurate machinegun fire killed at least 20 enemy soldiers and completely disrupted their initial attack. Pfc. Lozada remained in an exposed position and continued to pour deadly fire upon the enemy despite the urgent pleas of his comrades to withdraw. The Enemy continued their assault, attempting to envelope the outpost. At the same time enemy forces launched a heavy attack on the forward west flank of Company A with the intent to cut them off from their battalion. Company A was given the order to withdraw. Pfc. Lozada apparently realized that if he abandoned his position there would be nothing left to hold back the surging enemy soldiers and that the entire company withdrawal would be jeopardized. He called for his comrades to move back and that he would stay and provide cover for them. He made his decision realizing that the enemy was converging on 3 sides of his position and only meters away, and a delay in withdrawal meant almost certain death. He continued to deliver a heavy, accurate volume of suppressive fire against the enemy until he was mortally wounded and had to be carried during the withdrawal. His heroic deed served as an example and an inspiration to his comrades throughout the ensuing 4-day battle.

Pfc. Carlos James Lozada is buried at Long Island National Cemetery, Farmingdale, New York.

LOUIS R. ROCCO

Warrant Officer,
U.S. Army Advisory Team 162.
(1938–)

U.S. MILITARY
ASSISTANCE
COMMAND

Born in Albuquerque, New Mexico, November 19, 1938. Citation: WO Rocco distinguished himself when he volunteered to accompany a medical evac team on an urgent mission to evacuate 8 critically wounded Army of the Republic Vietnam personnel. As the helicopter approached the landing zone, it became the target for intense enemy automatic weapons fire. Disregarding his own safety, WO Rocco identified and placed accurate suppressive fire on the enemy positions as the aircraft descended toward the landing zone. Sustaining major damage from the enemy fire, the aircraft was forced to crash land, causing WO Rocco to sustain a fractured wrist and hip and severly bruised back. Ignoring his injuries, he extracted the survivors from the burning wreckage, sustaining burns to his own body. Despite intense enemy fire, he carried each man across approximately 209 meters of exposed terrain to the friendly perimeter. On each trip, his severely burned hands and broken wrist caused excruciating pain, but the lives of the unconscious crash survivors were more important than his personal discomfort, and he continued his rescue efforts. Once inside the friendly position, he helped administer first aid to his wounded comrades until his wounds and burns caused him to collapse and lose consciousness. His bravery under fire and intense devotion to duty were directly responsible for saving 3 of his fellow soldiers from certain death. His unparalleled bravery in the face of enemy fire, his complete disregard for his own pain and injuries, and his performance were far above and beyond the call of duty and were in keeping with the highest traditions of self-sacrifice and courage of the military service. Action took place N.E. of Katum, Vietnam, May 24, 1970.

EURIPIDES
RUBIO
Captain, U.S. Army, 1st Bn.,
28th Inf., 1st Infantry
Division.
(1938–1966)

Born in Ponce, Puerto Rico, March 1, 1938. Citation: For conspicuous gallantry and intrepidity in action at the risk of his life above and beyond the call of duty (at Tay Ninh Province, Vietnam, November 8, 1966). Capt. Rubio was serving as communications officer, 1st Battalion, when a numerically superior enemy force launched a massive attack against the battalion defense position. Intense enemy machinegun fire raked the area while mortar rounds and rifle grenades exploded within the perimeter. Leaving the relative safety of his post, he received 2 serious wounds as he braved the withering fire to go to the area of most intense action where he distributed ammunition, re-established positions and rendered aid to the wounded. Disregarding the painful wounds, he unhesitatingly assumed command when a rifle company commander was medically evacuated. Capt. Rubio was wounded a third time as he selflessly exposed himself to the devastating enemy fire with renewed effort. While aiding the evacuation of wounded personnel, he noted that a smoke grenade which was intended to mark the Viet Cong position for air strikes had fallen dangerously close to the friendly lines. Capt. Rubio ran to reposition the grenade but was immediately struck to his knees by enemy fire. Despite his several wounds, Capt. Rubio scooped up the grenade, ran through the deadly hail of fire to within 20 meters of the enemy position and hurled the already smoking grenade into the midst of the enemy before he fell for the final time. Using the repositioned grenade as a marker, friendly air strikes were directed to destroy the hostile positions. Capt. Rubio's singularly heroic act turned the tide of battle, and his extraordinary leadership and valor were a magnificent inspiration to his men.

Captain Euripides Rubio is buried at Buxeda Memorial Park, Cupey, Rio Pedras, Puerto Rico.

HECTOR SANTIAGO-COLON

Specialist 4th Class,
U.S. Army,
5th Bn., 7th Cavalry,
1st Cavalry Division.
(Airmobile).
(1942–1968)

Born in Salinas, Puerto Rico, December 20, 1942. Citation: For conspicuous gallantry and intrepidity in action at the risk of his life above and beyond the call of duty. Sp4c. Santiago-Colon distinguished himself at the cost of his life while serving as a gunner in the mortar platoon of Company B. On perimeter sentry duty, he heard distinct movement in the heavily wooded area to his front and flanks. Immediately he alerted his fellow sentries in the area to move to their foxholes and remain alert for any enemy probing forces. From the wooded area around his position heavy enemy automatic weapons and small-arms fire suddenly broke out, but extreme darkness rendered difficult the precise location and identification of the hostile force. Only the muzzle flashes from enemy weapons indicated their position. Sp4c. Santiago-Colon and the other members of his position immediately began to repel the attackers, utilizing handgrenades, antipersonnel mines and small-arms fire. Due to the heavy volume of enemy fire and exploding grenades around them, an enemy soldier was able to crawl, undetected, to their position. Suddenly, the enemy soldier lobbed a handgrenade into Sp4c. Santiago-Colon's foxhole. Realizing that there was no time to throw the grenade out of his position, he retrieved the grenade, tucked it in to his stomach and, turning away from his comrades, absorbed the full impact of the blast. His heroic self-sacrifice saved the lives of those who occupied the foxhole with him.

Sp4c. Hector Santiago-Colon is buried at Salinas Municipal Cemetery, Salinas, Puerto Rico.

M. SANDO VARGAS

Major, U.S. Marine Corps,
2nd Bn., 4th Marines,
9th Marine Amphibious
Brigade.
(1940–   )

Born in Winslow, Arizona, July 29, 1940. Citation: For conspicuous gallantry and intrepidity at the risk of his life above and beyond the call of duty while serving as commanding officer, Company G, in action against enemy forces (Dai Do, Vietnam) from April 30, to May 2, 1968. On May 1, 1968, though suffering from wounds he had incurred while relocating his unit under heavy enemy fire the preceeding day, Maj. Vargas combined Company G with two other companies and led his men in an attack on the fortified village of Dai Do. Exercising expert leadership, he maneuvered his marines across 700 meters of open rice paddy while under intense enemy mortar, rocket and artillery fire and obtained a foothold in 2 hedgerows on the enemy perimeter, only to have elements of his company become pinned down by the intense enemy fire. Leading his reserve platoon to the aid of his beleaguered men, Maj. Vargas inspired his men to renew their relentless advance, while destroying a number of enemy bunkers. Again wounded by grenade fragments, he refused aid as he moved about the hazardous area reorganizing his unit into a strong defense perimeter at the edge of the village. Shortly after the objective was secured the enemy commenced a series of counterattacks and probes which lasted throughout the night but were unsuccessful as the gallant defenders of Company G stood firm in their hard-won enclave. Reinforced the following morning, the marines launched a renewed assault through Dai Do on the village of Dinh To, to which the enemy retaliated with a massive counterattack resulting in hand-to-hand combat. Maj. Vargas remained in the open, encouraging and rendering assistance to his marines when he was hit for the third time in the 3-day battle. Observing his battalion commander sustain a serious wound, he disregarded his excruciating pain, crossed the fire-swept area and carried his commander to a covered position, then resumed supervising and encouraging his men while simultaneously assisting in organizing the battalion's perimeter defense.

MAXIMO YABES

First Sergeant, U.S. Army,
4th Bn., 9th Inf.,
25th Infantry Division.
(1932–1967)

25TH INF. DIV.

Born in Lodi, California, January 29, 1932. Citation: For conspicuous gallantry and intrepidity at the risk of his life above and beyond the call of duty. 1st Sgt. Yabes distinguished himself with Company A, which was providing security for a land clearing operation (near Phu Hoa Dong, Vietnam). Early in the morning the company suddenly came under intense automatic weapons and mortar fire followed by a battalion sized assault from 3 sides. Penetrating the defensive perimeter the enemy advanced on the company command post bunker. The command post received increasingly heavy fire and was in danger of being overwhelmed. When several enemy grenades landed within the command post, 1st Sgt. Yabes shouted a warning and used his body as a shield to protect others in the bunker. Although painfully wounded by numerous grenade fragments, and despite the vicious enemy fire on the bunker, he remained there to provide covering fire and enable the others in the command group to relocate. When the command group had reached a new position, 1st Sgt. Yabes moved through the withering hail of enemy fire to another bunker 50 meters away. There he secured a grenade launcher from a fallen comrade and fired point blank into the attacking Viet Cong, stopping further penetration of the perimeter. Noting 2 wounded men helpless in the fire swept area, he moved them to a safer position where they could be given medical treatment. He resumed his accurate and effective fire killing several enemy soldiers and forcing others to withdraw from the vicinity of the command post. As the battle continued, he observed an enemy machinegun within the perimeter that threatened the whole position. On his own, he dashed across the exposed area, assaulted the machinegun, killed the crew, destroyed the weapon, and fell mortally wounded.

Sgt. Yabes is buried at Fort Logan National Cemetery, Denver, Colorado.

SOURCES

America's Medal of Honor Recipients. Highland Publishers.
Current Biography Yearbook. The H.W. Wilson Company.
Extraordinary Hispanic Americans. Chicago Children's Press.
Famous Mexican-Americans. Dodd, Mead & Company.
Famous Puerto-Rican Americans. Dodd, Mead & Company.
Hispanic Business Magazine. Santa Barbara, California.
Hispanic Heroes of the U.S.A. EMC Corporation.
The Hispanic American. Meltzler, Milton, New York.
Vista Magazine. Coral Gables, Florida.
Who's Who Among Hispanic Americans. Gale Publications.

INDEX

INDEX BY OCCUPATION